A  Guy

When Your Normal Is Extraordinary

Matthew S. Miklasz

ISBN: 978-1-61244-682-0
Library of Congress Control Number: 2018960275

Printed in the United States of America

Halo Publishing International
1100 NW Loop 410
Suite 700 - 176
San Antonio, Texas 78213
1-877-705-9647
www.halopublishing.com
contact@halopublishing.com

To Jesus Christ. May this book result in praise to You.

Contents

Acknowledgments:

To the delight of my eyes, Cyndy: You are the picture of commitment, perseverance, and love. Thank you for never leaving my side throughout our journey. Thank you for believing in me and in this project. I love you.

To Angela, Benjamin, David, and Emily: You bring me great joy. I am so proud of who you are each becoming. I am honored to be called your dad. I've said it since you were all little, "Daddy loves you."

To Mom: You have always made me believe I could do anything. Thank you for caring so much. Yes, the dogs are fine. I love you.

To my crazy family: Deborah, Linda, Tom, Beth, and Mary — I am so grateful that God brought us together as a family. I love you.

To Dad and Mom V.: Thank you for all your love and support.

To John and Becky Milliren: I love your family. Your friendship with Cyndy and me means the world to us. Partner, I consider it a privilege to journey with you.

To Brett and Sarah Mayfield: Thank you for believing in me and in this book. Without your support, it's doubtful this book would have been written.

To Jordan and Sheila Skiff: We are so grateful for your love, laughter, and prayers.

To Tom and Chris Sigrist: Your names appear often in this book. I know and love Jesus better because of your investment in my life. Thank you. We miss you.

To Julie: Thank you for your kind heart and keen eyes.

To Elim Mission Elders and my church family: You didn't ask for a pastor with cancer. But you sure loved the one God brought to you. I thank God for you.

There are so many people who have impacted my life and it would be difficult to list all of them. So thank you to everyone who has impacted my life over the years.

Introduction

Why would anyone want to read what I write? That is the question I asked myself when my oldest daughter Angela encouraged me to write a book. I wear blue jeans and t-shirts most of the time. I drive a 1998 Ford F-150 pickup, and when I pull in the driveway I have to carefully avoid dogs and cats. What do I, a guy with bills and concerns about paying for my kid's graduation, have to say that could help someone?

What is there in my experience and abilities that could empower others? Why spend so many hours staring at the computer screen to create this testimony?

Here's why: I may be a normal and regular type of guy, but I know God has taught me so much and given me the ability to connect with other normal people. It is in this connection that God's voice has spoken to me about how our lives matter: why our normal matters. He has helped me to see that there are the lives we wish we had and the lives we really have. The disconnect between these two has prevented many people from living an impactful life.

I am not a CEO of a Fortune 500 company or an in-demand speaker. I am not a best-selling author (although that would be a nice result of this effort!). Who I am is a normal, regular guy who lives as authentically as I can, seeking to impact as many lives as I can along the way.

It is my sincere prayer that as a result of this book, you, the reader, are encouraged and challenged and that you gain confidence as you live your life in the day-to-day. In these pages are lessons from my journey, insights and applications offered from one journeyer to another. I'd like to thank you, the reader, for taking the time to consider what I have to offer in this book.

As a Christian, ultimately my identity is found in being God's child. However, no matter where you are at in your spiritual journey, I truly believe this book will provide many applications for your life along with help and hope for your future. I believe that deep down you want to live a life that maximizes your experiences, gifts, talents, personality, and passions. I believe you want to make a difference in the world where you live via the relationships you have. My goal in writing this book is that you and I will commit to a wholesale pursuit of maximizing our normal life.

This book is a reflection of a normal man's life. I will be honest with you about my journey in the hope that it will help you on your own rocky road. Believe me—my journey isn't always pretty, but I want to be authentic in sharing because it's at this level I feel I can give the most encouragement. This is not a self-help book. But I do hope it helps you, the reader. Much of what I have written is reflective and contains many lessons I have journalized throughout my life. I also focus on the application of principles and truths that will help us be aligned with who God created us to be. I especially hope you are able to find the joy of discovering and becoming your "normal" more and more.

About four years ago, God led us as a family to Cokato, Minnesota, to lead a church. When we first arrived, I regularly met new people. Knowing I was a pastor, one of my new acquaintances said to me, "You know, you're just a normal guy." I wasn't quite sure what to do with that statement. He seemed surprised by his discovery. It surprised me when again, I heard that word used in reference to me. My family, especially the one I grew up with, certainly wouldn't say I qualified as normal!

As I reflected on these comments, questions surfaced.

* What did the people making these statements mean by "normal"?
* Why did I not know if I was being complimented or insulted?
* Should I be acting in a different manner or presenting myself more professionally?
* Had I been too casual with people?

The thrust of this book is that being "normal" is being the real you that God created you to be—you glorify Him more fully when your life is aligned with who He created you to be. As we will discover, our normal, when lived out, is extraordinary.

CHAPTER ONE:

Choosing a Reliable Lens

"Your word is a lamp for my feet, a light on my path."

Psalm 119:105

I have deep convictions about this "normal" way of life. The first is that it is of the utmost importance that we use the right lens in order to see reliable answers. Whenever I go to get new glasses, I take an eye test that reveals the type of lens I need. Having the right lens is necessary if I am to improve my vision and see images clearly. The same is true in life. If we are to see ourselves and our lives truthfully, we need the correct lens. If we use the wrong lens, we will have a distorted view of ourselves, our purpose, and reality.

What lens will you use to answer these questions?

* Can you have confidence in life?

* Is your life aligned with who you are created to be?

* What is this normal life that I am referring to? What does it look like? How will it impact lives?

Merriam-Webster gives us a working definition of the word normal.

Definition of normal. *1 a: according with, constituting, or not deviating from a norm, rule, or principle. b: conforming to a* *type, standard, or regular pattern. 2: occurring naturally and not because of disease, inoculation, or any experimental treatment.* [1]

The phrases "according with" and "not deviating from" in the definition hit at the heart of what I am saying. We must ask, "In accordance with who?" "Not deviating from what?" Is the lens of culture a reliable standard with which to answer these question? Will this lens give us the clarity that leads to freedom and confidence? Does God have something to say on the issue? If so, is God's Word, the Bible, a reliable lens?

With regard to our identity, normal is not referencing a rule, norm, or standard. We are talking about a design. That design is God's creation. He created you with a specific design. So it only stands to reason that we would use the Bible as the lens to see who we really are and to define our normal. In keeping with Merriam Webster's definition, we are to live "according to" our design—our normal. We are not to "deviate from" our normal. Your normal is not my normal, but both of our true identities are worth celebrating.

We live in a culture where an enormous amount of energy and resources are exerted in order to be anything but "normal." Think of the commercials you see. Notice how the advertisers pitch you the idea of being noticed for what you wear, or unfortunately, in some cases, for what you don't wear. The implication is that being "you" might not be enough. We are being told that we need a little more charisma, education, a larger portfolio, or greater positional significance to be somebody worthwhile. Anyone who comes across as normal when compared to the cultural standard is considered boring, settling for a life that is wasted. Every day, society makes a value statement about people. Namely, that individual value is linked to culturally adopted characteristics such as age, physical attributes, athletic talents, and financial security. If someone doesn't measure up, the conclusion is that this person is normal, with the attached implication that they are less desirable and lack potential. That may be culture's lens and society's mindset, but it is not God's.

I believe the Bible is God's Word to men and women. I will reference it often, for within its pages we are able to find the wisdom of God, and we can't top that for reliable direction.

I am intrigued by a passage from the Bible that is used in reference to the apostles, Peter and John. The situation in the New Testament book Acts, Chapters 3 and 4, centers around a concern about a man who has been healed by the apostle Peter. After being healed, this man goes, of all places, to the Temple, the center for religious activities, to rejoice in his new ability to walk. Peter and John have also been preaching the good news: that Jesus has died and risen from the dead providing salvation for all who believe. These activities caused great alarm to the religious leaders of the time, who felt threatened by Peter and John. Thousands of people were placing their faith in Jesus. So threatened were the religious leaders that they had the two seized. They hoped to intimidate them through their interrogation. I am sure there were expectations that these two men, Peter and John, would be impressive, gifted, and influential men, considering the kind of impact they were having. The ability to speak to a man and heal him, along with having thousands respond to your speaking certainly puts you in an elite class. What an impact! Obviously, these must have been highly educated and skilled orators. That is probably what the leaders were expecting.

We too would expect to read that Peter and John were neatly dressed, well organized, and highly motivational. But that is not what the text tells us. Instead, we read the conclusions of those who interviewed Peter and John: "When they saw the courage of Peter and John and realized that they were unschooled, ordinary men, they were astonished and they took note that these men had been with Jesus" (Acts 4:13 NIV).

As I studied this verse, the word "ordinary" jumped off the page. These men, after being observed by the religious establishment, were found to be uneducated and ordinary. Really? They had just preached to a crowd of thousands of responsive people. They were responsible for healing a man, and the conclusion is that they were "ordinary"?

From some earlier verses, we know that the Holy Spirit had come to dwell in these men, filling them with a new power that accompanied their speaking and actions. To me, this highlights a key point. God chose to use "uneducated and ordinary" men. God did not wait for Peter and John to get a degree, develop certain leadership traits, or gain a certain religious status. He used them as they were, in alignment with who they were; He empowered them. Remember—*that* is what it means to be normal. I can't emphasize enough how significant this is.

As we look at our lives through God's lens, we find that our normal indwells God's story. It's in Christ that we find out who we are. We find podcasts, self-help experts, talk show hosts, and myriads of other voices sending us toward self-discovery. But they send us in the wrong direction, using the wrong lens. When we begin with God's lens what we discover is nothing short of extraordinary.

Chapter Two:
A Beginning Toward My Normal

"For we are God's handiwork, created in Christ Jesus to do good works, which God prepared in advance for us to do."

Ephesians 2:10

I have a deep desire to impact lives. I know it's the many small decisions I make, the actions I take, that together add up to determine whether I have lived and loved well on any given day. To say it takes intentionality to maximize a normal life would be an understatement. Each day we make choices, set priorities, and pursue goals that either result in living below our potential or in bringing about real growth.

The choices we make today have been influenced by many people, experiences, lessons, and failures in the past. First and foremost, the greatest influence in my life is Jesus Christ. As a student at Luther College in Decorah, Iowa, I heard Jesus call my name. Between being recruited to play football and the beauty of the campus, my parents decided that Luther was a good place for me to study.

In observing the lives of a couple of guys with whom I played ball, I saw purpose, joy, and fulfillment—all of which were absent from my life. Their lives were magnetic.

A word that could sum up my life at that point was "lost." I was lost in every way imaginable. This manifested itself in a pursuit of fulfillment centered on experiences. I thought sports would certainly bring the fulfillment needed to fill my life and bring me clarity. But when practice ended or the scoreboard clock read 0.00, even if we won the game, I was still very lost and empty.

I had a lot of relationships but very few friends. The drinking scene offered more dissatisfaction. I wasted time and money on alcohol, coming to the realization that I was surrounded by people who were as lost as me. I was searching, and it seemed most of the people I hung around with were not honest about what was going on in their lives. They offered me no help in my search.

I had a cleaning job on campus in a building called, if I remember correctly, The Center for Faith and Life. When I had accomplished my tasks, if time remained on my shift, I was given the freedom to do homework. One of the guys with whom I played ball invited me to attend a Fellowship of Christian Athletes (FCA) gathering held in the building where I worked. I wasn't clear on what "fellowship" meant and fuzzy on the name "Christian", but "athlete" I knew. So I thought I'd check out the gathering. The atmosphere of the gathering impressed me. I observed a warmth and genuineness that allowed me to relax. When the gathering ended, after I had met some of the attendees there, for some reason, I signed up for a Bible Study. (It had to be easier than college Biology and German—I hated those classes.)

During the week, I received a call from a guy I had met at the FCA gathering. He gave me the details of where the study group would be held. I had forgotten I had signed up, and I had to decide if I wanted to go. Apprehensively, I attended. The group began with a study on who Jesus Christ is and why He came to earth. I was given a guide—the Bible. I read the verses listed and answered the questions. I'll be honest; it took me forever to find the references as I did not know the Bible and I was ignorant about the books within it. I had grown up going to church but never chose to crack open a Bible. I knew and believed that God existed and created this world. I knew about the coming of Christ as a baby. I heard about His death and resurrection but I was not sure what that meant to me.

Through this study on the life of Jesus Christ, I learned how He fulfilled over 500 prophecies in His coming to earth. I learned that He lived a perfect life. That He died to pay for my sins and rose from the dead, providing abundant and eternal life for me. The Bible told me that my sin had separated me from God. Growing up, I thought of God as a distant deity who was not really interested in me. After all, He had a lot on His plate. Yet, the Bible talked about having a relationship with God.

I can only describe what happened as my eyes were opened. I saw that Jesus is the Savior of the world and that if I wanted to have a relationship with God, I needed to trust in Jesus Christ's death and resurrection on my behalf. My good works would never be enough to make me right with God. I needed to be forgiven and I needed a new heart. As I walked back to my dorm one night, I went to a little chapel on campus. All alone, I knelt on the floor and I asked Jesus Christ to save me. The peace and reality of God's presence were unmistakable to me as I walked out of that chapel. I knew God had done something within me. He had changed me. I knew Jesus had now come into my life. An awareness that I did not have before became present in my life.

For example, I had never worried about what I said, how many f-bombs I dropped, or whether someone would be hurt by my words. All of a sudden, there was an awareness and an ability to curtail my speech that I hadn't seemed to have before.

I had never concerned myself with how much I drank or whether it was wise or not. I now evaluated the party scene in a new light. I remember fraternity initiation night. The challenge that had been issued required me to go around the town, stopping in all the bars, with the expectation that I would kiss a certain number of girls. That isn't something I would normally do, to say the least, but alcohol removed my filters and led to me acting like someone else. My behavior was not aligned with who God created me to be.

My point is not to get on a soapbox about the consumption of alcohol but to highlight that God created you and me with our distinctive personalities, passions, gifts, abilities, and temperaments. I began to discover that the party scene was moving me away from aligning my life with who God created me to be, my normal. In keeping with the premise of this book, when I was drinking I was not conforming to my normal. No wonder the author of Proverbs writes: "Wine is a mocker, strong drink a brawler, and whoever is led astray by it is not wise" (Proverbs 20:1 ESV).

After giving my life to Christ, I realized that I could enjoy being with friends and not getting drunk but actually trying to get to know the people I was with and hearing their stories. I found the freedom to try to understand how I am wired and what I care about. I could see the foolishness of looking to activities and people to fulfill my life. Moving away from the party scene was primarily about obedience. A directional change became necessary. I was moving toward a lifestyle that allowed me to flourish in my growth and understanding of who I was. Changing my foul language and partying habits are examples of what I mean when I say "aligning our lives with who we were created to be." Clearly we were not created to live carelessly but purposefully.

Shortly after trusting Jesus Christ as my Savior, God gave me a deep desire that I had not felt before to pray and study the Bible. God was changing me, and although there were hints, it would take a while before I began to discover and align myself with who God created me to be. I love Jesus for many reasons, certainly because He loved me and died for me, making it possible to be with Him forever. But to know that He wants to have a relationship with me is staggering. I mean—the God of this universe saw something in me that He valued enough that He died for me. I came to the conclusion that I mattered to God and that I needed to discover my identity. I knew that I had many facades. I realized that it takes a lot of energy to be someone you're not—doesn't it? My priorities were all centered on me. Believe me, there is no fulfillment in trying to be the center of all things. I did not know how to love people. I knew how to use and manipulate them, but I knew very little of what it meant to sacrificially love someone.

During Jesus' life here on earth, a man once asked Him a question, "Of all the commandments, which is the most important?" Jesus answered him with these words, "The most important one is this: 'Hear O Israel: The Lord our God, the Lord is One. Love the Lord your God with all your heart and with all your soul and with all your mind and strength.' The second is this: 'Love your neighbor as yourself. There is no commandment greater than these'" (Mark 12:29-31 NIV).

The first part of Jesus' commandment is easy to understand. We know what He is saying. God is to be the highest aim of our affections. There should be no rival to our love for Him. Questions arise about what He means in the second part of the statement.

*What does it mean to love my neighbor as myself?

*How do I or should I love myself?

I suggest that Jesus is saying that we should love who God created us to be, our normal, and to love others as they have been created to be. There is no selfishness or pride implied. I believe Jesus is making a statement about valuing our neighbors. In Jesus' words, we find the vertical and horizontal orientation of our faith with regard to expressing love. If we love God, that love will naturally overflow toward our neighbors. However, it is very difficult to truly love others when you aren't sure who you are or what it looks like to love another person "as yourself."

The journey that I began in college and continue to pursue to this day is to live out being who God created me to be and to do it in a way that pleases Him. I believe this pursuit can have a positive impact on others around me. Little did I know back in 1983 what a journey this would be and the challenges this would present.

To live the normal life that has an incredible impact is to begin by trusting Jesus Christ as Savior. He created you and calls you to a relationship with an ongoing experience of being used by Him. The normal is maximized when you live with your personality, gifts, talents, and passion, allowing God to transform you for His purposes. You could say that this is your unique calling. I believe

God has a call for each of our lives. A call to live for Him, to love, and to serve others. I elaborate on this more in a later chapter.

I was encouraged early in my Christian walk to record my faith journey. My friend suggested that I record the times God spoke to me through His Word and circumstances. I chronicled encounters that had a profound impact as well as conversations that contained insights I believed God wanted me to write down. I began the habit of writing down these insights on a regular basis. I have many journals that I revisit and reread to remind me of God's work in my life and the lessons He has taught me— lessons that He wants me to continue to apply today.

The Bible teaches that when someone trusts Christ as their Savior, God gives His Spirit to indwell that person. I can testify to the Spirit's work, leadership, and voice in my life. The Holy Spirit enabled me to see what lay beneath the surface of my life. The entries in my journal form a composite of who I once was and who I am now in the process of becoming. The Holy Spirit helps me see what I need to see. There were things I didn't see in the past, and now, as I look back with what I have learned, they seem obvious.

I believe being normal includes the perspective Abraham Heschel wrote about in his book, "Man is Not Alone: A Philosophy of Religion." Heschel writes, "Our life is not our own property but a possession of God. And it is this divine ownership that makes life a sacred thing." [1]

To be normal is to live with the conviction that you belong to God, and when you align yourself with that reality, the impact you can have is absolutely staggering. Consider that the God that spoke the world into existence is not limited in any way. This certainly includes how and to what degree He can use us. He created you and me to be uniquely normal and to align ourselves with that reality which will allow us to have an extraordinary impact on the world. The following chapters will provide practical ways to discover and align your life with your normal.

CHAPTER THREE:

Recognize the Value God Places on You

"Our lives are a collection of stories—truths about who we are, what we believe, where we come from, how we struggle, and how we are strong. When we can let go of what people think, and our own story, we gain access to our worthiness—the feeling that we are enough just as we are, and that we are worthy of love and belonging. If we spend a lifetime trying to distance ourselves from the parts of our lives that don't fit with who we think we're supposed to be, we stand outside of our story and have to hustle for our worthiness by constantly performing, perfecting, pleasing, and proving." [1]

-Brené Brown

Many of us have experienced feelings of inadequacy. There are times when we do not seem to measure up. Charles Schultz always did a masterful job of capturing these common feelings in his cartoon character, Charlie Brown. Charlie Brown, Linus, and Lucy are lying on a hillside looking up at the clouds. Lucy says, "If you use your imagination, you can see lots of things in the cloud formations. What do you think you see, Linus?"

Linus replies, "Well, those clouds up there look to me like the map of British Honduras on the Caribbean. The cloud up there looks a little like the profile of Thomas Eakins, the famous painter and sculptor. . . And that group of clouds over there gives me the impression of the stoning of Stephen. I can see the Apostle Paul standing there to one side."

Lucy responds, "Uh-huh. . . That's very good. What do you see in the clouds, Charlie Brown?"

Linus was a tough act to follow.

We are people who like to compare, but this often results in feelings of insignificance. We see larger-than-life athletes, gifted film directors, and movie stars. Even as I am writing this, I am reminded of the great books I have read, and I feel intimidated. We are quick to assess our value in comparison to someone else. Let's face it—we struggle with a sense of value at times. Consider the rapid technological advancements. We are quickly becoming numbers and statistical units rather than meaningful individuals.

Growing up, I worked at a bakery in Crystal Lake, Illinois, owned by some friends of ours. It was a great job that only intensified my love of donuts. A cake donut with chocolate icing has got to be a foretaste of heaven! When customers entered the bakery, they needed to take a number to be served. They would tear a number off a roll and wait for their number to be called so they could place their order. In the bakery, they were a number, not a name. In our world, we too feel like a number. I think that's why I like to address waiters and cashiers by their name listed on their nametag. It seems more personal and communicates value to them. I hope, even to a small degree, they feel noticed as not just a face but as a whole person. I think that's why I enjoy waiters and servers who take the time to ask my name. I feel valued when someone takes the time to do this—and I'm sure to tip this person well once the meal is over! I really believe that all people need to understand the great value they have.

I am so thankful God gave us the Bible to tell us the truth about our worth. I like what former president Ronald Reagan said, "Within the covers of the Bible are the answers for all the problems men face." God's Word offers life to our soul. The Bible offers the solution for the restlessness in our souls. What the Bible communicates about our significance in the Creator's eyes nourishes my soul.

The first book of the Bible, Genesis, declares that human beings are made in the image of God. "Then God said 'Let us make man in our image, according to our likeness, and let them rule over the fish of the sea and over the birds of the sky and over the cattle and over all the earth.' And God created man in His own image, in the image of God. He created him; male and female He created them" (Genesis 1:26-28 NIV).

Our worth is connected to our Creator. If God is of great and inestimable worth, then human beings made in His image must be of great value. Of no other being created does God ever say they were created in His image. Only human beings. The fact that we are made in God's image provides the basis for our work and vocation, our recreation and all of our lives. If we are made in the image of God, we share some of His characteristics. For example, because God is creative, we can be creative in our work, and in fact, we are called to such creativity. God is wise and therefore we are able to obtain wisdom, albeit to a much lesser degree.

Also, knowing the basis for our dignity and worth helps us believe that we have gifts and talents to employ. I know many people who haven't discovered their calling because they don't believe they have anything to offer. They don't believe they have dignity and worth, and as a result, they fail to recognize their God-given gifts. Being normal starts with understanding our worth and our value to God. We cannot be who we were created to be unless we know that the One who created us sees us as significant—of great value. To be normal, we need to know that deep down we matter. Greg Stine, a Christian comedian, once said in his routine, "When the God of all matter says you matter, that's self-esteem." I believe that!

Science hasn't helped humanity understand our value. Some scientists view our universe as being vast, so vast they've concluded that the earth is insignificant. A speck of matter surrounded by galaxies. The immensity of creation, as it continues to be discovered, has us revisiting certain questions in our own lives, especially questions of our significance. I just read in the newspaper about a young man who committed suicide. I weep and wonder if he knew he mattered. That God created him for so much more. Yesterday, a female pop star overdosed on heroin and almost lost her life. While she is famous for her music, I wonder if she believes she matters aside from her music. This young lady needs Psalm 139. We all need Psalm 139.

Psalm 139, from the Old Testament, is a revealing biblical passage, illuminating the significance of each person's value. What is revealed is nothing short of amazing and profound in its implications. The psalmist who we know to be David, God's chosen leader of His people, writes:

You have searched me, Lord,
and you know me.
2 You know when I sit and when I rise;

you perceive my thoughts from afar.
3 You discern my going out and my lying down;
you are familiar with all my ways.
4 Before a word is on my tongue
you, Lord, know it completely.
5 You hem me in behind and before,
and you lay your hand upon me.
6 Such knowledge is too wonderful for me,
too lofty for me to attain.
7 Where can I go from your Spirit?
Where can I flee from your presence?
8 If I go up to the heavens, you are there;
if I make my bed in the depths, you are there.
9 If I rise on the wings of the dawn,
if I settle on the far side of the sea,
10 even there your hand will guide me,
your right hand will hold me fast.
11 If I say, "Surely the darkness will hide me
and the light become night around me,"
12 even the darkness will not be dark to you;
the night will shine like the day,
for darkness is as light to you.
13 For you created my inmost being;
you knit me together in my mother's womb.
14 I praise you because I am fearfully and wonderfully made;
your works are wonderful,
I know that full well.
15 My frame was not hidden from you
when I was made in the secret place,
when I was woven together in the depths of the earth.

16 Your eyes saw my unformed body;
all the days ordained for me were written in your book
before one of them came to be.
17 How precious to me are your thoughts, God!
How vast is the sum of them!
18 Were I to count them,
they would outnumber the grains of sand—
when I awake, I am still with you.

Psalm 139:1-18 (NIV)

I believe this passage is a balm to the heart and mind of anyone who struggles with feeling insignificant or insecure. Maybe, deep down, you have questions about whether you really matter. Maybe you've been abandoned by a parent or a spouse, rejected by an employer, or turned down by a college, and you find the idea that you don't have much to offer seeping into your mind. Perhaps you are wondering if people are right to reject you. Please don't believe that; it's not true. You have great value, and recognizing that is a huge step toward being normal; being the you God created. If you are wrestling with the issue of your significance and worth, here is a psalm just for you. Psalm 139 describes a person who is standing alone and searching for answers about himself, his world, and his God. This psalm leads us to some questions.

Verses 1-7 of Psalm 139 address the question of "how well does God know me?" In verse 1, the word "searched" in Hebrew literally means, "to explore; conveys the idea of digging into or digging through something." The thought is that God explores, digging into you and examining you thoroughly. His creation of you wasn't a chance thing. He formed you and me very specifically so that we could realize our normal.

God searches, not because He doesn't know, but because we don't know how well He knows us. Look at verses 2-4. We are told that God is completely familiar with our most common and casual moments, like sitting and rising. He is completely familiar with everything, not some or most, but all of your ways. Not only all of your ways but also all of your thoughts.

In verse 3, the psalmist writes, "You perceive my thoughts from afar." Thoughts come into our minds through a series of distant, fleeting conceptions as microscopic nerves relate to one another in the brain through a complicated series of connections. Even these are known by the Lord.

Have you ever seen thoughts come into someone's mind by observing their facial expressions? I was watching my son playing a video game last night, and as he sat playing the game, there was a point in the game when he was trying to capture the enemy. As he got close to the enemy, his expression registered the thought, "I am not going to get the guy." I could read the thought from his expression. So we can get an idea of what people may be thinking. But we don't see what prompts their thoughts. God does. He understands the hidden, unspoken thoughts and motives behind our actions.

God carefully examines our choices, and He is thoroughly acquainted with us. In theology, we use the word "omniscience", and in simple terms, it means that God knows everything—all of our thoughts and even the words that will come out of our mouths before we utter them. Think about it: God knows every word of every language in every human being on every continent at every moment of every day. That is a big God!

According to a passage in the New Testament, God knows the "very hairs on our heads" (Matthew 10:28-35 NIV). That is amazing, although I admit it was much more impressive when I was younger and had more hair. God is all-knowing, fully and accurately aware of all things at all times.

How well does God know you? He could not possibly know you better. If you are feeling insignificant, ponder the fact that the living God is paying attention to you at every moment. This blows the psalmist's mind, as he says in verse 6, "Such knowledge is too wonderful for me, too lofty for me to attain." The psalmist's questions about value begin to fade away as he realizes God views His creatures as significant.

Why does this matter? Think about this. God is not some distant, preoccupied deity. He is all-knowing and present everywhere. We need to know how exact His knowledge of us is. This is comforting, for even though He knows everything about us—all the sin, rebellion and the secrets—He still sends His Son Jesus to die for us. He is always with us! Whatever you face this week, God will be with you for He has already been there. He knows you and what you will face. So call out to Him daily! You are valuable to the God of the universe.

As a believer in Jesus Christ, the Bible says I have been brought near God by the blood of His Son Jesus, and now, I can approach God's throne which is marked by grace. I can find help and hope. The testimony of the New Testament book Hebrews states, "Let us then approach God's throne of grace with confidence, so that we may receive mercy and find grace to help us in our time of need" (Hebrews 4:16 NIV).

Over the years, I have heard people say something along the lines of, "I don't think my prayers are getting past the ceiling."

The reality is they don't have to get that high; God is in the room with you. Your parents may have failed you, and your friends may have belittled you, but God Almighty has created you and breathed life into you. He wants a relationship with you, which is evidenced by His intimate knowledge of you!

The next time you are outside on a clear night, look up at the stars. Look long enough to allow your mind to grasp the immensity of the galaxy above. Remind yourself that you are more valuable and significant to God than any of the stars and planets put together.

This is the conclusion the psalmist reaches, writing, "I praise you because I am fearfully and wonderfully made; your works are wonderful, I know that full well. My frame was not hidden from you when I was made in the secret place" (Psalm 139:14-15).

The psalmist, David, breaks forth in praise. You and I are creatures of wonder, knit together in the womb by God. No one would argue that the human body is an incredible combination of physical strength, beauty, coordination, and grace. We haven't even begun to discuss what the heart, mind, and spirit are like.

Several years ago, Sam Speron, MD concluded that:

* You lose around 50-100 hairs from your head every day, but they are replaced that same day.

* Around 45 miles of nerves run through your body. These electric impulses travel at speed of almost 250 mph.

* The air from a sneeze can reach the speed of 100 mph.

* A square of human skin contains 20 feet of blood vessels, 1300 nerve cells, 100 sweat glands, and 3 million cells.

* Each second 10,000,000 cells die and are replaced in the body

* The liver is the body's chemical factory. It has over 500 functions.

* The average human body contains enough: sulphur to kill all the fleas on an average dog, carbon to make 900 pencils, potassium to fire a toy cannon, fat to make 7 bars of soap, phosphorous to make 2200 match heads, and enough water to fill a ten-gallon tank. [2]

Amazing doesn't begin to describe how wonderfully we are created. The cure for feelings of insignificance and poor self-image is not to start with the self but with God. He carefully knitted you together in the womb; He knows you intimately and cares for every area of your life. He loves you completely! I remember reading somewhere that the great Bible teacher Donald Barnhouse once said that the most profound verse in all the Bible is, "For God so loved the world that He gave His one and only Son that whoever believes in Him shall not perish but have eternal life."

It sure helps me realize my worth when I remember that Jesus died for me. I also remind myself that He died for my neighbors, my acquaintances, the teenagers I coach, and the people I encounter on a daily basis. I think we too often forget the value of everyone around us.

"The awe that we sense or ought to sense when standing in the presence of a human being is a moment of intuition for the likeness of God which is concealed in his essence," wrote Jewish scholar Abraham Heschel. "Not only man; even inanimate things stand in relation to their creator. The secret of every being is the divine care and concern that are invested in it. Something sacred is at stake in every event." [3]

"Something sacred in every event." That should slow us down when we look at our encounters with those around us in this way. Every dinner with our family, going on a walk with a friend, chatting with a neighbor—these become moments where valuable people spend time together. It is significant because all are made in the image of God. If we could remember that and treat one another accordingly, we'd have a whole lot more smiles and a lot less despair.

I spent some time today with a family helping them clean up their house so they could sell it. As I was cleaning the horse barn out, sweeping up the horse and chicken poop, I began thinking about what a joy and privilege it was to help this precious family. You see, their daughter's health has been declining. Doctor after doctor can't find a way to bring relief from all the pain. She has lost so much weight and she has become so fragile. However, this young lady is incredible. She has an infectious smile and a huge heart. I know Cyndy, my wife, would agree that to help this family is such a privilege. Is it too much to think that something sacred took place in the barn earlier today? Could the value I place on this family and the relief I longed to provide for them in some way reflect the image of God? I think so.

On the way home, I stopped at the grocery store. At the checkout, a grumpy woman (don't worry, I called her by her first name anyway) begrudgingly rang me up. I confess, my appreciation of her value was not what it should have been at that moment. I wonder how I could have expressed to her that I recognized she had great value. That someone cared, amidst the frustration of her day. It's not always easy to know the best way to do that, but I know I need to be reminded often to treat people well because they are valuable.

Some years ago, the varsity coach of the local high school asked me to assist a first-year basketball coach. She was a very energetic young lady who enjoyed coaching. She was a tad hesitant to listen to this 48-year-old man who had been asked to assist her. During one of our first practices, I shared with her that one of the most important things she could do as a coach was to learn the names of the custodians. She looked at me with an odd expression. I explained that they work hard behind the scenes, preparing the gymnasiums for practice. They needed to be affirmed and recognized for doing so, not taken for granted. If she would do this, the players would also recognize the custodians' value and hopefully it would carry over into how they treated their teammates. I fear she didn't get the lesson. I hope you do!

Being normal is about knowing you have great value and so do those around you.

CHAPTER FOUR:

Value Your Family

*Our families provide a link to our yesterdays
and a bridge to our tomorrows.*

-Matthew S. Miklasz

I want to begin this chapter by letting you know I am sensitive to the fact that some of you grew up in homes that did not have two parents, or you may have had relatives serving as your guardians. In some cases, maybe there were unhealthy relationships that affected your home and the atmosphere where you grew up. Perhaps you experienced abuse or your parents divorced or there were other unhealthy dynamics at play. You need to know I am thinking of you when I write this chapter. Your stories are probably very different than mine. Your stories are a part of who you have become. I am sure your experiences have forged and continue to forge great convictions. The good news is that no matter how hard our younger years were, through His power and His Word, God can provide us a new start and a new family legacy. You can begin a new chapter in your family that can extend into generations. Now that is an impact, and yes, God can use you to do that!

I would like to share about my family growing up because those relationships impacted me and are a part of who I am today. So as I recall specific times and lessons I hope they will spur you on to reflect on your family's relationships and history. I am so grateful for the family that I had growing up: my dad and mom and four sisters and one brother. I was the second youngest child. We had so much fun, and now, we have even more fun. My parents modeled and communicated the importance of our family. So much of who we are comes from the influence and nurture of our families. So we would be wise to consider our families as we consider our normal. I have some moments etched in my mind of times with my dad and mom. I vividly remember a picnic where my dad and I walked away from the crowd to the end of a boat dock. We sat and talked for quite a while. We didn't talk about anything in specific; we were just together. With six kids and long workdays, one-on-one time with Dad came at a premium.

When in high school, my dad decided to move from Illinois to rural Wisconsin. Dad had found some property with an old barn on it. His plan consisted of turning the barn into a new house. So, over the next two years, we made trips on weekends and spent more time in the summer working on remodeling this barn. It was hard work, but I enjoyed learning from Dad.

He seemed to take delight in risking my life with some of the jobs that he handed over to me. One day we were working on painting the barn. One of the peaks was so high that even the fully-extended extension ladder, placed on a pickup, could not reach by about six feet. I know because Dad had me try. We moved the ladder around to the other side of the house where we could get on the roof. Dad decided that if he tied a rope around my ankles, he could lower me over the edge to paint the peak. So that's what we did. I was hanging upside down with a paint can and brush painting the peak while all my blood rushed to my head. I got the job done, but I'm pretty certain any safety department wouldn't have appreciated our plan.

Dad was constantly accepting antennae tower jobs, and all of these jobs required someone to risk their life. That was namely me. He didn't like heights so he figured I would.

After we moved to Wisconsin from Crystal Lake, a city west of Chicago, I learned that in Wisconsin no one picked up your garbage. We had to actually take it to the dump. So, Dad and I, who are both well over six feet tall, and my very short Uncle John, would go take a load of garbage to the dump. If you remember the movie *Twins* starring Arnold Schwarzenegger and Danny Devito, you'll have an image of what my dad and Uncle John looked like together. We'd have so much fun.

I know this may sound weird, but I love to go to the dump. I especially like bringing the kids with me. I think a part of me remembers how fun those times were when I was going up. We spent time together laughing and talking, and that was enough.

Dad was a strong man and a good model of masculinity. He had a John Wayne aura about him, which is why I think Dad loved his movies. We all grew to love those movies as well. I even do a pretty good John Wayne imitation.

Growing up, I learned that a man must take care of his family. He must take his responsibility to provide for them and protect them seriously. A man should be honest, hard-working, and reliable.

As we got older, I believe Dad grew in communicating his love for us. It was probably in my mid-20s that I began to notice every phone call with Dad ended with him saying, "I love you, son." I don't remember hearing that much growing up. I knew Dad cared, but I didn't hear him say it very often. I miss hearing him tell me that; it meant so much to me. My dad passed away five years ago to the day I am writing this chapter. I miss him and often think of the times we shared. In certain situations, I still find myself asking "what would Dad do?" I am blessed to have had him as my dad.

I resolved to let my children know I love them when I tuck them into bed and drop them off at school. I regularly tell them I love them, and I never want them to doubt that. I feel that when I tell them I love them in the morning, I leave them with words that can follow them through the day and bring them comfort and confidence. I am glad my children seem to be making efforts to communicate love. My oldest daughter Angela is good at ending phone calls by telling me she loves me, while Emily just tells me at random times. I don't think my children will ever know how much that means to me. The boys are a little slower at doing this, but it took me a little bit to learn it too.

My siblings and I had a healthy fear of Dad and we knew if we were rebellious, especially if we made things hard for Mom, we'd get the belt. Mostly we were given what I call a "Dad-ism" You may remember some of these "Dad-isms" from when you were growing up. They always came with that different tone. Here are some I remember.

* Because I'm your father. . .

* When I was a boy. . .

* I used to walk 8 miles to school every day. . .

* You want your allowance—you know where the mower is.

* I will break every bone in your body.

* You call that hair combed?

* You want something to cry about? I'll give you something to cry about.

* Tom, I mean Beth, I mean Linda. . . whatever your name is, come here. Now!

* I will knock a fart out of you that will sound like a buzz saw.

I believe in appropriate corporal punishment. I know it's almost culturally taboo, but I don't care. Children grow up more responsible and respectful when they have parents who love them and lovingly spank them. We are seeing increasing amounts of disrespect in our culture, and I know it sounds simplistic, but a little spank on the backside and soap in the mouth would help with that.

A popular online video recently showed a dad making his young son walk home from school in the rain because the boy had bullied a classmate. As the dad slowly followed the son in his car, he videotaped his son walking in the pouring rain. The comments underneath the video demonstrated the prevailing cultural mindset. Several people verbally attacked this dad and claimed parental abuse. I laughed and wanted to high five the dad. To me, that's good parenting as long there is also encouragement, many hugs, and "I love yous" at home.

When there is punishment without love, that's abuse. Healthy discipline begins and ends with love. Love does not allow a child to behave in a way that is harmful to others and to the child as well. Actually, this brings us back to the previous chapter about valuing other people. Often, when I was spanked it was because I didn't value other people and I deserved to be spanked.

My mom is the strongest woman I know. Her perseverance and will are unbelievable. My mom had a stroke when I was little, and we almost lost her. She recovered but was unable to regain the use of one arm. Her speech didn't return easily either. She worked hard with the therapists to get stronger and recover her speech. She had great motivation to get strong to take care of our family. I didn't see the improvements as clearly as my older siblings, but I remember seeing improvement. She learned to do so much with one hand; it still amazes me.

My mom did something growing up that I am so grateful for—it became our special time together. When I came home from school, I would sit at the kitchen table and she almost always sat there waiting. I would have a snack and tell Mom about the day. She'd listen to me share about my day. I always felt that I was so special to Mom.

I read an article from the magazine *Higher Perspective* in a clinic recently and found the following. "Did you know that: talking to your mother has the same effect as a hug and can help reduce stress levels? The sound of her voice releases oxytocin and is great stress relief."

I find that true in my life. When I call Mom and talk with her, the world seems a little more bearable and my challenges not so difficult. It is quite humorous to talk on the phone with Mom, as she always asks first about our dogs, even before checking on the rest of us. She sure loves animals. One of God's greatest blessings to me is my mom, and whatever perseverance I may have has been modeled by her.

Grandma Becker, my mom's mother, was a significant part of our family as well. She was kind, loving, and funny, and she always seemed happy to see us. We spent a lot of time playing cards with her. I treasure those memories of all of us being together during the holidays. Returning to the simplicity of the moments that you treasure helps ground you.

My siblings are wonderful. I could not begin to share how diverse, goofy, and loving they are. When we get together, there is much laughter. My kids comment how fun it is to be with my family. Each of us is unique, and together we become a comedy show. The book of Proverbs says, "Laughter is medicine to the soul." Well, my siblings and I sure take a lot of medicine. One time, my oldest sister called me out of the blue and said, "I called because I need to laugh, and you always make me laugh."

We seem to handle stress and grief with humor, so much so that we almost got kicked out of my grandpa's funeral visitation. The funeral home in Chicago had about six to eight different viewing rooms. With so many rooms holding visitations, any commotion would potentially be a disturbance. Along with our cousins, we just made each other laugh so much that we couldn't stop. We meant no disrespect, but that is a picture of how much fun we have and how humor helps us deal with loss. In my early 20s, I took my family for granted. I sure don't do that now. I look at other families and how shallow their relationships are or how non-expressive they are and become even more grateful.

When I officiate at a funeral service, I make sure to encourage families to recommit to and appreciate each other. If necessary, I encourage them to be quick to forgive each other.

I am sure my family has been disappointed in other family members at times, but we verbalize our concerns and move on. We are a family who expresses our love through hugs and words. When we grieved together through Dad's final, difficult years, I think it brought us even closer. It is hard to leave my siblings after a visit.

When I was diagnosed with colorectal cancer (cancer of the colon and rectum), my siblings were so supportive. My sister Mary sent me all these cards with butt jokes, and they provided a needed smile in the midst of chemo and radiation treatments. This shows that we laugh so we don't cry at times. When I had my cancer surgeries, all my sisters came to the Mayo Clinic to be with us. Seeing them after waking up from surgery was the best medicine I could have possibly received. I have pictures of my sisters visiting me in the hospital, and I love what these pictures communicate to me. They tell me I am richly blessed by such incredible support.

While we joke as a family, we don't cross the line to careless and cutting remarks. I think that it's very sad when families bring each other down or speak to each other in condescending ways. Our home should be the place where we get built up and encouraged the most. I praise God for my family and appreciate how close we are. They bring a lot of sunshine into my life, especially during some of the dark and uncertain days. I hope that wherever your family relationships are that you work on strengthening them. Don't take each other for granted. Be quick to forgive each other. Be patient and loyal. Express your love to one another. Your life will become that much richer. Tell someone in your family how much you appreciate them. Give them a hug if they are close by.

Go ahead; I'll wait for you. Okay, how did that feel? You probably don't fully know how much that meant to your family member. Please make it a priority to actively express love to your family.

My sister Mary posted a picture of us on Instagram from my hospital room at the Mayo Clinic, and she put a caption that said something like, "He stays so positive." That meant a lot to me because I really try to do that and she took the time to affirm what she saw.

When Cyndy and I began seeing each other, we quickly learned that our families were really different. I think that the fact that I am a hugger came across as a little odd to Cyndy's family but I wore some of them down and they will give me a hug now. They are a very supportive family and a huge blessing as well.

Cyndy and I waited about five years before we started to have children. It proved to be a good decision as we used this time to focus on deepening our relationship. Cyndy is amazing. One of the things I have loved since we first met is how authentic she is. She doesn't try to pretend to be someone else. She is both very adventuresome and very practical. I am kind of a visionary and sometimes I am way out in front of things. Cyndy is able to bring me back to the moment. Her commitment to me has been unwavering.

With us moving as a family a couple of times over the years, and through the demands of my cancers and church ministry, Cyndy has always been there to support me and believe in me. Over the years, it has meant so much to hear her say, "You're a good pastor," when I didn't feel like a good pastor. Throughout the many years I have served in the ministry, there have been very difficult seasons. Cyndy has stood with me, supported me, trusted me, and believed in me. There were many times I didn't believe in myself, times I didn't trust myself or my decision-making, but she did. At times, I have wrestled with loneliness, and while I am good at concealing it, I think she senses those times and encourages me to contact a friend or family member.

I love being married to the delight of my eyes. The heightened joy of having children together only enhanced our relationship. What a beautiful and intimate experience to have children. I remember the three times I have been in the delivery room. What always caught my focus during the deliveries of my children was their beautiful mother.

I remember the excitement when our first child Angela came into the world. She was the first grandchild on Cyndy's side and she sure got spoiled, especially by Cyndy's dad, "Papa." On my side of the family, she was the youngest grandchild, who seemed to have a special bond with my dad, "Poopa." My children are very blessed in that they have wonderful grandparents, uncles, and aunts. I hope they remain grateful.

My sons, Benjamin and David, are really different from each other in temperament and giftedness. They are both entering their senior year of high school. My desire for them is that they be normal; that is, to be who God created them to be. I want Benjamin and David to be confident in who they are and to be fearless men of God. I hope they become men who look at life through the lens of God's ability and not man's inability. I want them to choose to speak words that bring life to other people, not words that destroy or damage others. I want them to love Jesus and His church. To know, deep in their souls, that the church is Christ's instrument to reach the world. I want them to be committed to each other as a family. I want them to leave a legacy of godliness.

A couple of years ago, Benjamin and David had to face a real possibility that if cancer took my life, they would have had to, as I told them, "be the men in the house." This last year, I have seen real maturity in both of them, and I feel confident that should something happen, they would be able to shoulder the responsibilities of helping to provide for Cyndy and take care of things. My boys are way smarter than me and also more creative. I am encouraged that Ben and David both have the ability to persevere.

After Ben's birth, the nurse came and took him from us in the hospital room to clean him up. Soon, a doctor came to our room and told us there was something wrong with Benjamin's heart. He would need to be flown by helicopter to a children's hospital. We knew his condition was serious. It was apparent by the doctor and nurses' demeanor that there was urgency to get him to a children's hospital. Cyndy and I wept when the nurses let us see him before he was taken to the helicopter. As he was positioned in an oxygen bubble, our nurse asked if she could take our picture with Ben. So, next to his bubble we took the picture. It was hard to smile. The picture shows us with red eyes along with Benjamin in the oxygen bubble. They would end up flying him to the children's hospital in Milwaukee where he would have open-heart surgery. Cyndy said she felt good enough to leave and the nurse checked her out and let her go home. My wife is tough! So we ran home and packed before catching a couple hours of sleep. Early the next morning, our friends Roger and Sharon drove us to Milwaukee.

At five days old, Benjamin had open-heart surgery, and he pulled through. We were in Milwaukee for almost a month. I never left and I am grateful to the Faith Ev. Free Church in Stanley, Wisconsin, who understood that I had to suddenly leave. Since then, Ben has had a procedure at nine months old and two open-heart surgeries, one when he was 9 years old and one when he was 13. We pray that he is done being opened up for any more surgeries.

Our son David came to us by adoption from Ethiopia. God brought him to us at approximately 5 years old. He has had to adjust in more ways than I can even comprehend—to a new family, a new community, and a new country. We have also had to move a couple of times, which is a hard enough adjustment, and each time, he has had to walk into a predominantly white community as a young black man. He has shown an amazing ability to be flexible and integrate which I admire. I am very proud of my two sons and I love them to pieces. I am so excited to see how God uses them in the years to come.

My daughters, Angela and Emily, while different, also have some similarities. (Although the thought that they are similar right now would be traumatic to them.) They are both independent and hard-working. I am very proud of their work ethic. Our families have a strong work ethic and we see that in our kids. As I look around the landscape of America, the thought of working hard is foreign to many. If you have young children, please give them chores. Make them earn some things so they know that not everything will be handed to them. My girls know the value of hard work. Both Angela and Emily are also very good with people. They get energy from being with people and they have many friends.

My daughters have a lot of love to give and I am glad they are so caring and expressive. I knew, when it came to raising daughters, I needed help. This awareness resulted in reading a lot of parenting books to find insights and little behaviors to implement. The one thing the books and seminars can't teach you is the depth of the love between a dad and his daughters. It is unique and it can't be replaced. Angela and I enjoy sports together. Emily loves her horses so it is fun to experience some of her shows and competitions with her.

One of the greatest experiences in my life was after one of my cancer surgeries. Angela and I went to Chicago, where we stayed in an apartment in Wrigleyville and went to see a couple of Chicago Cubs baseball games. We ate Chicago food, which consists of the greatest sandwich ever made—specifically an Italian beef sandwich, hold the peppers. During the Cub's world series run, Angela and I were texting each other throughout the games, sharing our nervousness. We do the same with other sporting events as well. Angela is the one child who spent the most time at practices while Cyndy or I coached teams. She has been around sports since she was a baby.

Emily and I are planning to go to big horse competitions in Las Vegas. She will make sure I don't forget that. She is mature beyond her years. I just love being with my girls. I also know I have missed many opportunities to contribute to their lives and that grieves me, but I am working harder on seizing all the opportunities I can.

I am highly protective of my girls, and they know I will not just give my permission to any man to date them. So they better wait until there is a quality guy. Just between you and me, when I visit Angela at college and meet any of her male friends, I always give a little extra squeeze on the handshake so they know there is more where that came from should they mess with my girl.

I know it's not culturally sensitive to speak of my daughters as my "little girls" or say that they need protecting, but I don't care. I am seeking to be daughter sensitive, not culturally sensitive.

As a dad, I clearly recognize that sons and daughters are different. God created them differently, and that is to be celebrated, not minimized. When she was younger, Angela was helping me lay block for an addition that we were putting on our house. Late in the day when we were finishing up, she asked me, "Dad, what do I get for helping with the work today?" I asked her what she wanted and she said she wanted to play Barbie Uno with me. I still tear up when I remember that. My boys would never ask to do that with me.

We need role models that are confident in who they are. I am so blessed to hear testimonies of stepfathers and stepmothers who have willingly brought a father's or a mother's heart into their new family. I believe there is a call to grandparents to fill in the gap for fatherless or motherless grandchildren. That call has never been greater. There are many young children that I see on a regular basis who have no real fatherly love poured into their lives. Our young girls and boys need strong male and female role models or they will grow to be confused and ultimately frustrated. In my pastoring, coaching, and volunteer opportunities, I try to communicate to young girls and boys that they are valued and loved.

If God created you to be a male, celebrate that and grow in that. If God created you to be a female, celebrate and grow in that. I feel that in training our children, whether at home or in the church, there needs to be a renewed emphasis on what biblical masculinity and biblical femininity are. God's design cannot be improved upon, and it is to our detriment to mess with it. For you and me to grow in discovering our normal, we need to be appreciative of and confident in our masculinity or femininity.

Here are some applications for all of us to live out our normal life. First, I believe you and I should value our family by prioritizing them. Secondly, commit to spending more time together and engage in regular conversation. Thirdly, avoid letting anger and bitterness linger in family relationships. Maybe it's time to forgive or let go of past hurt. Don't be like so many people who hold a grudge and let bitterness eat away at their relationships with their family. At funeral services, I witness families whose loved one is lying in the casket and they can't get past a disagreement from years ago. Finally, I believe love is meant to be expressed and we should seek to express our love in fitting ways. Learning from our family relationships and experiences brings greater clarity in discovering our normal.

I believe hugs are a great way to express our love. They are more significant than we realize.

Years ago, I wrote down something in my journal that I saw posted on the wall at Milwaukee Children's Hospital. It stated that touch is very important for development and bonding. It went on to say that studies have shown that positive touch can:

* Slow heart rate

* Lower blood pressure

* Help regulate breathing

* Improve weight gain

* Lower stress hormones

* Decrease pain levels

* Facilitate bonding

With just those benefits alone, why would we not hug and give positive touch to one another? Hug your family often. I am a hugger and I am proud of it. According to author Paul Planet, I am a health nut. He writes:

> Hugging is very healthy. It helps the body's immune system. It keeps you healthier. It cures depression and reduces stress. It induces sleep. It is invigorating. It is rejuvenating. It has no unpleasant side effects. Hugging is nothing less than a miracle drug. Hugging is all-natural. It is organic and naturally sweet. It contains no pesticides, preservatives, or artificial ingredients, and it is 100% wholesome.
>
> Hugging is practically perfect. There are no movable parts and no batteries to wear out, no periodic check-ups, no monthly payments, no insurance requirements. It offers no energy consumption and returns a high-energy yield while being inflation-proof, nonfattening, theft proof, non-taxable, nonpolluting, and fully returnable. [2]

Cyndy and I try to keep our home a positive environment. It is my hope to see a consistent atmosphere developing that is marked by love, laughter, hugs, and encouragement. I believe as each member in our homes lives aligned with their normal, our families can become that much richer.

I want to encourage you to value each other's strengths and learn to laugh at your mistakes. Develop within your family a safe home filled with a lot of laughter and expressions of love and appreciation. If your home situation seems hopeless, begin by taking one step at a time toward a healthier environment. I know if you make these efforts there will be a positive change, and you'll take great strides toward seeing the impact of a normal life.

CHAPTER FIVE:

Appreciate Your Memories and Experiences

"Everybody needs his memories. They keep the wolf of insignificance from the door."

-Saul Bellow

Our minds are truly amazing. The ability to remember is a great gift. Our memories can retain satisfying and joyful experiences of people, events, and circumstances. There may also be random information such as the words to the Gilligan's Island theme song that linger in our minds. The opposite is also true. We can remember hurtful, traumatic, or fearful experiences.

I feel for those whose memories are filled with painful experiences. When in conversation with people in pain, my spirit becomes heavy with grief, and I long to bring relief. Memories can be so raw, and although an event may have happened many years in the past, there are triggers that can make it real again. Counseling offices and mental health facilities are filled with precious people who can't seem to come to terms with, or process in a healthy way, those memories that hold them in bondage. I believe that in those extremely painful moments, God can heal us, turning these moments into something that can help others. I have met many people and read about many more who have come to a place where they recognize that their traumatic experiences have provided a way to come beside and help others.

I have concluded that our memories can produce an avenue for personal growth and discovery if we steward them well. For many years, I have used a journal when I read my Bible. This discipline serves as a guide and a way to remember all the ways God has spoken to me. This also serves to remind me that He has worked in my life and through my life. The memories of my walk with God encourage, remind, and warn me. They bear witness to my convictions. They are an important part of who I am and what my normal is.

Reading through a couple of older journals last night, I came across lessons and insights that I had actually forgotten. Much of it provided great encouragement, reminding me that God had, in simple moments of my life, worked in and through me. I am currently spending a year reading through the Bible, and I just finished a chapter in the Old Testament book of 2 Kings. As I read through my journal, I came across an entry of my thoughts on that same passage from 1999. There were insights into that passage that had been tucked back in the recesses of my mind. My journal brought those insights into the forefront and, in that way, my study in 1999 provided teaching for me once again. This is the great value of memories. If we let them, they will teach us.

Many have said experience is the best teacher. I don't believe that's necessarily true as stated. I believe the lessons applied from experiences provide the best teaching. If we don't apply what we have experienced, we waste our experiences because we are not drawing from our memories.

A conviction of mine is that God does not waste anything. For example, when I was about 10 years old, I experienced a weird episode while playing Monopoly with my family. I got disoriented and sick. I tried to go to the bathroom, but I could not focus, talk, or even respond. (Perhaps this is why I hate Monopoly). I had to be taken to the hospital where I was diagnosed with a seizure disorder.

From the age of about 10 all the way through my last one at 35 years old, I have experienced seizures. I have had seizures on a pontoon boat, in motel rooms, in the bathroom, and even under a tree in Mexico. I guess I like variety. So what do all the memories of these experiences teach me? The main lesson is one I have needed to learn repeatedly throughout my life, namely, that I am not in control of my life. There are things I have control over and responsibilities I have, and my decisions are real decisions with real consequences and outcomes. What my seizures and the circumstances surrounding them have taught me is that God is in control of my life. Should I think differently, I need only to remember all the times I have had seizures and recall that it was completely out of my control to stop them. With almost every seizure, I bit my tongue severely, often to gross extremes that would affect my speech for several days.

I often speak to groups and, of course, to my congregations, and should I be tempted to think God needs me to speak, I think back and realize the only reason I *can* speak with clarity is because God allows me to speak. It really is that simple. If I take this to its most basic point, the only reason I have breath is God has allowed me to.

Another lesson I have drawn from the memories of those seizures is that God can use them in other people's lives. When I took a youth group to Mexico on a mission trip, we embarked on an incredibly long trip to get there. It was blistering hot.

Even though I was wearing a hat and drinking a lot of water, the heat triggered a seizure. I was taken to a hospital back in Texas; the ride was horrible and the hospital worse. The hospital's air conditioning had broken down. My room was very hot and I knew, based on past experiences, that I needed to cool down and take a certain medication to settle things down. The staff at the hospital secured neither a fan or the necessary medication. It wasn't until I had another seizure that the staff took my condition seriously. Hours later, I returned to the compound back in Mexico and got some sleep. The seizures had sapped my strength for the next couple of days. What did happen during this time was that a young man on the trip named Jason stepped up and took real leadership of the group.

The circumstance of my seizures put Jason in a position where leadership was needed. He had to step up and help move the group forward to be able to accomplish the objectives our team. I was able to use the experience to help Jason see how gifted he is. Sometimes experiences force us, and others, to step out and do things they never dreamed they were capable of. Jason now runs his own business, coaches athletics, and has a beautiful family. He also has a memory of when his leader fell ill and he had to step in to fill the void. So memories teach those who are part of the circumstances. This article by Susan Krauss Whitbourne emphasizes the connection of memory, learning, and our identities:

> Our identities become shaped by our life stories as we gradually incorporate the memories of the events in our lives into our sense of self. The most important of these, the "self-defining memories," are the ones that we

remember most vividly and that contribute most heavily to our overall sense of self. A self-defining memory is also easily remembered, and emotionally intense. In some cases, these memories represent ongoing themes that we play out over and over again in our lives. Learning to recognize your own self-defining memories can help you gain important insights about your identity.

Whitbourne goes on to point out,

> In an intriguing study, Connecticut College psychologist Jefferson Singer and his colleagues (2007) compared older adults with college students on self-defining memories. They found that older adults tended to come up with more general memories that linked several events together and that, in general, older adults tended to feel more positively about their self-defining memories, even if the memories were of events that were negative in nature. These findings fit with other lines of research suggesting that older adults have found ways to make sense out of their life stories. They convert memories of troubling events into stories of redemption in which they make peace with their past struggles. For younger adults, events of a negative nature had more rough edges, causing them to experience greater distress when they recalled them... This means that the more you are able to talk about the meaning you derived from an event, the more likely it is that you'll be able to grow and elaborate your sense of identity. [1]

You'll notice Whitbourne's article repeatedly mentions the connection between memories and self-identity and growth. The article also points out the significance of the meaning we attach to a given memory. The article mentions an interesting insight: that older adults have the ability to process difficult memories in a way that fits in with their stories. I believe this to be true and would attribute it to having learned to appreciate the value and the lessons that memories can provide. We would be wise to let our memories and experiences be our tutors.

Our memories don't just exist in a vacuum, nor are they static, for many testify to the power of the emotions that are attached to memories. Our senses can also trigger the power of memories. I believe both the emotions and the senses that are attached to our memories have much to teach us.

I remember lilac bushes we had in our backyard growing up. The two bushes were planted next to each other, and there was a small opening between them that my sister and I would go into, pretending we were in a spaceship. Standing in our lilac bush spaceship, we were engulfed by this beautiful fragrance. I love the smell of lilacs. To this day, the smell often triggers my memory of two children enjoying a ride in a spaceship that looked and smelled like a lilac bush. This quote was tucked into one of my journals, and it reiterates how attached our senses and our memories are:

> Nothing is more memorable than a smell. One scent can be unexpected, momentary and fleeting, yet conjure up a childhood summer beside a lake in the mountains; another, a moonlit beach; a third, a family dinner of pot roast and sweet potatoes during a myrtle-mad August in a Midwestern town. Smells detonate softly in our memory like poignant land mines hidden under the weedy mass

of years. Hit a tripwire of smell and memories explode all at once. A complex vision leaps out of the undergrowth. [2]

"Memories explode all at once," Ackerman writes, and we know this to be true. It does appear there is often a necessary step we need to take of separating the emotion from certain memories so we can derive the lesson from the experience. Learning can be stifled if we can't get past the power of the emotion. Even the most difficult of memories is an opportunity to learn so much when we take the time to process them. When the memories are so intense that they can overwhelm an individual, it is wise to seek a counselor.

Some years ago, I was having a very difficult season in my life. I was becoming depressed, which intensified the loneliness I have sometimes faced. My church district superintendent encouraged me to see a Christian counselor who had graciously made himself available to pastors. This counselor provided the help I needed. He helped me to unwind the ball of emotions I had been suppressing. He talked me through the memories that were attached to those emotions. I had suppressed emotions surrounding my dad's dementia, strains in my relationships, and frustrations in church. At times, seeing a mentor or a counselor is a very courageous thing to do to help ourselves. At that point, I needed to heed the advice I had given over the years. Counseling is not a sign of weakness, unlike what we can be led to believe.

Learn to appreciate your memories and experiences. They will help you discover your normal and give you direction in aligning your life with your normal. Unwrapping our memories and discovering the many lessons contained within is a lifelong process.

One of my favorite television shows from some years ago is *The Wonder Years*. The show portrays a family living between 1968 and 1973. I loved that this show made memories surface and the dynamics of the characters relating to one another. Each episode would end with a brief narrative that often contained a good lesson. One such episode ended with a narrative that said, "Memory is a way of holding onto the things you love, the things you are, the things you never want to lose." Hold onto your memories and appreciate them. They teach us a lot about how to live a normal life.

CHAPTER SIX:
Live Positively

"The longer I live, the more I realize the impact of attitude on life. Attitude, to me, is more important than facts. It is more important than the past, than education, than money, than circumstances, than failure, than successes, than what other people think or say or do. It is more important than appearance, giftedness, or skill. It will make or break a company. . . a person. . . a home. The remarkable thing is we have a choice every day regarding the attitude we will embrace for that day. We cannot change our past. . .we cannot change how other people will act. The only thing we can do is play on the one thing we have, and that is our attitude. . . I am convinced that life is 10% what happens to me and 90% how I react to it. And so it is with you. . . we are in charge of our attitude."

-Charles Swindoll

We cannot live a life aligned with who God created us to be if we don't place God in the equation of every area of our life. An awareness of God's presence in our lives brings perspective. The word "enthusiasm" comes from the Greek word "entheos", which means God within or God in. Living positively means that we understand God is in it. This is where we learn to see circumstances and experiences through the reality that God is not only aware of what we face, He has allowed what we encounter in life. When we believe and act upon those truths, the enthusiasm that will appear in our lives is amazing.

The significance of a positive attitude cannot be overstated. It is paramount to living an impactful life. Those who know me best consider me to be a very optimistic person. Even in moments of frustration, I have also been described as "annoyingly positive." I'm not sure I have always been this way. I do know that when I trusted Jesus Christ as my Savior, He began to make changes in my life and I believe this is one of them. While it is easy to tell someone to "be positive", I think people need to be specifically shown how to adopt a positive attitude. Make no mistake: your attitude is your choice.

If I want to be my normal, I need to live positively or I will drift to a defeated mindset and settle for a lesser version of myself. We live in a very negative world. Just turn on the news and you'll see stories of death, murder, political scandals, cheating athletes, and addicted celebrities.

I believe it would be refreshing and make a noticeable difference if we were to turn on the news or read reporting on the internet that only focused on positive events. Only positive journalism for one day. Think about what it would be like to only hear stories about charitable acts, athletes overcoming obstacles, business executives making wise choices, and employers treating employees kindly. Just for one day—no negative stories or commentaries. Only positive focused media. It would lift people's spirits and it would invite others to enter into a tone of positive dialogue.

God thinks we are wonderful. He loves us very much. He knit us together in our mother's womb. He not only created us but also sustains us. He has not only made us gifted but can also empower us. He can improve our lives, even when we go our own way and make horrible mistakes. He still makes something good. He can take a life that is spent in the garbage dump of sin and make something beautiful. I find all of that incredibly positive. The author of Romans, who wrote to Christians, asks a rhetorical question, "If God is for us, who can be against us?" The answer is that no one who resists us or attacks us or has malice toward us can infringe in any way on God's affections for us and His goodness toward His children. I find that incredibly encouraging. As I like to say, it "gets the juices going." Now I recognize it's one thing to say "be positive" entirely another thing to live positively.

I specifically titled this chapter "live positively" because it's a daily choice we must make. I've often heard the expression "stay positive." That's not helpful, as there is a real chance that you or I might not be feeling or thinking positively at that moment. We cannot stay positive if we are not in that mindset. At times, we need a new beginning.

I want to share some specific and intentional strategies that help me to live positively. These past four years, with two cancer diagnoses, chemotherapy, radiation treatments, and several surgeries, I have been tested. Each day I faced new challenges and frustrations, but I knew I wanted to live positively so I chose to face it all, thinking of all the blessings from God and how He could use this in other people's lives. How can we live positively? The following are intentional actions I strive to apply that contribute to my pursuit of living positively.

Feed Your Mind That Which Is Good

Have you ever watched a movie or a show and when it was finished, you felt agitated? There are several movies and shows that I choose not to watch because they take my mind in a negative direction. One such movie came out years ago, in which a young boy is left behind by his unknowing parents as they scramble to reach their flight connection on time for their holiday trip. The movie begins showing this young boy acting like a disobedient snot. He is disrespectful and foul-mouthed. Watching him agitated me to the degree that I was ready to fly out to Los Angeles and spank the brat myself (well, not that agitated). The disrespectful and negative behavior of the young boy ruined the movie for me. I won't watch it anymore.

Other TV talk shows, while helpful to some on the show, regularly broadcast a degrading, disrespectful, and rebellious portrayal of humanity. The show doesn't help me to have a healthy outlook. Clearly, the tone of the media is perpetually negative, critical, and slanderous.

I find this is also true regarding music. Right now, a lot of music that is being released is dark and degrading. That doesn't help anyone live positively. I am sure you're like me, and when you're in a store or flipping through radio stations, you hear a song you know and the words come back to you. Soon you're caught up in the beat (by the way, nothing could top the music from the '80s in that department). Eventually, the meaning of the lyrics dawns on you. They have been stuck in your mind for years, but if you continue to feed your mind unhealthy words, your mind and emotions will follow suit.

Personally, I listen to predominantly Christian music or artists that I know typically have uplifting lyrics. Find music with lyrics you can trust. This will help you have a positive outlook on life.

The same is true with regard to what you read. Recently, I was waiting in the doctor's office for my appointment and I picked up a magazine. I flipped through the pages of celebrity gossip, and it didn't take long for me to set the magazine down, frustrated by the foolishness I was reading. I even caught myself talking to the magazine and communicating my displeasure! That frustration only increased with the realization that I was the one who had picked up the magazine in the first place.

I believe that social media can provide good opportunities to communicate with distant friends and families. I use it in that way. I am a little more cautious now, having recently observed people I know communicating in careless ways. It is disheartening to see the result. It would be much better and more redemptive to look at the good in others and, when there are concerns, go to that person and share these concerns. Unfortunately, some choose to be hurtful, but to live positively means choosing better behavior. Intentionally choose to watch, read, and listen to that which will help you become a better person. I am not too proud to admit that, unfortunately, at times, I have struggled with my thought life. The truth is that it is difficult to be consistently victorious when our culture is in the wholesale pursuit of violence, immorality, and degrading behaviors.

I have found that confessing my failures in this area and being accountable in choosing a better path has helped me in this battle. What we feed our minds matters, and for us to be our normal requires taking intentional steps. This leads me to my next intentional step toward living positively.

Reflect Before Reacting to Circumstances and Situations

Living positively doesn't mean that you and I keep our heads in the sand and ignore life's unpleasant situations. What it means is that we approach unpleasantness in a more positive and productive way. It means thinking that the best is going to happen and not the worst. It really starts with self-talk. Self-talk is the endless stream of unspoken thoughts that run through your head. These automatic thoughts can be positive or negative. The key is to respond in the moment in a way that is positive, not negative. When we resist reacting immediately, it gives us the time to adjust our self-talk.

Like each of the intentional behaviors I am outlining here, this doesn't come naturally. Our sinful self often seeks to react to what we encounter in unhealthy and destructive ways. For example, you're driving and get cut off by another motorist, or another driver doesn't use their turn signal (a pet peeve of mine). Our initial reaction is often one of anger, frustration, and—in extreme cases—seeking revenge. On the news (remember I mentioned it's often negative), I just saw a story about a driver who reacted with road rage toward another driver. When the vehicles stopped, the driver assaulted the man in the other car. How sad is that! Sure, maybe the one driver was careless, but perhaps it was because they really didn't see or were reacting to another driver's actions. If we can slow down our responses, we can often better understand a situation and even learn from it when we reflect on what happened. Ask questions like, "What good could come from these circumstances?" Or "What are the consequences if I lash out?"

For many years I struggled with frequent severe infections, and then, in 2012 I was diagnosed with leukemia. Then came colorectal cancer, and in both cases, my reaction was to pull away from everyone and fight it alone. The more I reflected on the situation, the more I became aware that I had an opportunity to show my family and church family how to persevere through hardships. Through my reflections, I saw that I needed to be more aware of what legacy and what resources I was leaving for my family. My reflections led to a more positive mindset and better behavior choices.

Consider another situation you might face. You get into an argument with your spouse, child, or sibling. You're starting to get angry or frustrated. In the past, you have reacted by yelling or saying hurtful words. If, however, you can choose in the moment to slow down, read the situation, and think first, you could begin to understand the other person's point of view. In my case, I often just wind up finding another reason to laugh at myself.

I have discovered that my pride is deep-seated, and it manifests in an attitude that hates being wrong and that comes out when I react to circumstances. When we reflect in the moment, we have opportunities available to us that are not there when we react immediately. We can avoid conflict and the wasted energy that brings. We can also potentially turn a very difficult situation by diffusing the emotion that is threatening to damage others. I don't always do this well, however, I strive toward responding in patience, understanding and loving actions.

Speak Well of Others

It is surprising that when focusing on the positive in others, the negative and critical fades. Part of my philosophy in coaching is to discover what each player does well and lock in on what that is. I affirm the player's strengths and try to put them in situations where they can succeed. I pursue this goal relentlessly. I have seen players blossom in regard to their self-esteem and confidence because someone believes in them. Now I might not put them in the game for 90% of situations, but the 10% of situations I do put them in the game, they come to believe they can succeed and expect to succeed.

This all begins with telling each player "good job" or "you're killing it today"—something that builds them up. By doing this, I see the players' strengths more than I see their weaknesses. I gain more of a positive attitude and outlook about that player and the team as a whole. I have coached each of my children in basketball, and they each have discovered certain things they do well. I helped identify those strengths and found ways to build on them. Instead of getting frustrated with my children, I talked with them about what they do well. This is exceedingly important in parenting. It makes a big difference to parent our children this way.

At times I see in myself, and in the parenting style of others, the mindset that if I browbeat my child, they'll shape up. However, that's not true. Instead of shaping up, they will shut down and you'll lose opportunities, perhaps forever, to build them up and help them believe that all things are possible.

When married couples come to me for counseling, there is often a tension that has resulted in a very narrow focus. The focus of each individual is on the other and their failures that have in their minds caused the problems they have. This narrow focus creates a negative atmosphere, making it difficult to work through the issues they are facing. In fact, the original issues become secondary compared to the atmosphere they have created. There is some surprise when I tell couples they are both responsible. An assignment I give them is to speak only positive things to and about each other for one week. One week only speaking positive things. I have not had one couple come back and say it was easy. Nor have I had a couple come back and say that it was not helpful. Negativity stifles growth while living with a positive focus fosters growth.

It can be so easy to adopt a negative attitude about people. At times, I think about my self-talk and cringe at what I say to myself about people. In each case, it's because I looked at what the other person did wrong or what I perceived as a personal slight toward me, and my mind gets negative.

I want to encourage you to intentionally think of ways to speak well of people. Remember there are an awful lot of negative things they could say about you. No one has it all together so there is no need to look for evidence of that; instead, point out qualities you appreciate or actions you saw as helpful and positive in the outcome. Make it your goal each day to affirm some trait or action in another person that you appreciate. If you do this, you'll be surprised by how your outlook will become more positive. I double dog dare you to take me up on that.

 Record Moments Where You Experienced God and His Goodness To You

This is an exercise that I have done in my journals, and it would be an understatement to say that I have been encouraged by rereading what I wrote down. God has been so good to me. Yet in the seasons of challenges and difficulties, I find it easy to forget.

I remember during my radiation treatments and chemotherapy regime how discouraged I started to get. One evening, I picked up some photo albums that Cyndy had put together—I looked at them over and over. The pages were filled with precious people that I am grateful to have in my life. Just picturing their faces helped lift me from the downward slide toward discouragement.

Living positively can be challenging, and for some, it may seem impossible. I have an incredible privilege to be a pastor and I am overwhelmed that God would choose me to help shepherd His people. I believe that part of my calling is helping people live positively.

In the midst of a very trying time at a church where I pastored, I worked hard to help people see that God could use the challenges we faced and that we could be stronger if we walked together through them. I sought to help people move beyond their unmet expectations and disagreements, choosing instead to focus on what God wanted to do in the moment. There were some, however, who would choose not to look past their own perspective, opinion, or preferences. They simply chose to be resistant to changing to a more positive mindset. Many of these folks hadn't recorded any of the moments when God showed up and changed their situation from their journey. The times God provided, healed, or comforted laid dormant in their minds. So, when challenges and conflict arose, they had very little to draw from. It is a lot like putting money in a savings account; you can draw some out when you need it. When we look back and draw out recorded moments from our journeys, we are able to keep God in the equation of our circumstances. When we do that, we can't help but be positive that everything will work out.

⌢ Enjoy the Gift of Laughter

The Bible promotes laughter and a happy heart. Laughter is referred to as medicine and it is presented as a gift to be enjoyed.

"A cheerful heart is good medicine,
but a broken spirit saps a person's strength."

Proverbs 17:22

"A joyful heart makes a cheerful face,
but with a heartache comes depression."

Proverbs 15:13

"For the despondent, every day brings trouble;
for the happy heart, life is a continual feast."

Proverbs 15:15 (NIV)

I have not seen anyone dying of laughter, but I fear that I do know many who are dying quickly because they are not laughing.

Charlie Chaplin was an English actor, comedian, and filmmaker whose work in motion pictures spanned from 1914 until 1967. During his early years in film, he became established as an engaging and funny actor. Interestingly enough in the 1910s and 1920s, he was considered the most famous person on the planet, according to Wikipedia. His life is perhaps best summed up by this quote: "A day without laughter is a day wasted." There is a lot of truth to that.

Life can be funny. I heard this story from a friend. One warm summer evening, a mother was driving her three young children, when a woman in a convertible pulled ahead of her and stood up and waved. She was stark naked! As the mom was reeling from the shock, she heard her 5-year-old shout from the back seat, "Mom, that lady isn't wearing her seatbelt." Admit it—you smiled at that.

At times in my counseling opportunities, I have actually counseled people to rent *Father of the Bride* or another comedy. I know that doesn't sound like a real remedy. But think about it— what do we need during times of difficulty and life's upheavals? We need perspective and relief or we'll get overwhelmed. The movie *Father of the Bride* communicates the value and richness of relationships. It reminds the viewer in a realistic way that life can be funny. It also sends the message that life is meant to be satisfying in the various experiences and seasons of our relationships. It is just good therapy to laugh together. Seriously, can you not laugh at Martin Short as Franc? I am laughing as I type this. Enjoying the gift of laughter is an important component of living positively.

Start Out Each Day Right

Living positively becomes reflexive when we set ourselves up for success. One way we do this is to begin each day well. When I was growing up, my mom and dad stressed the importance of having a good breakfast. They told us that it helped us get ready for the day. (Although when my dad made his "boat anchor waffles", we had trouble even getting out the door.) I still believe that eating a good breakfast is important. Breakfast is my favorite meal and I enjoy meeting people for breakfast. I know there are a lot of diets out there. I am not into counting calories, but after eating a good breakfast, I do have a light lunch.

Actually, I did find a stress diet I like.

Breakfast: ½ grapefruit, 1 slice whole wheat toast, 8 oz. skim milk

Lunch: 4 oz. lean boiled chicken breast, 1 cup steamed zucchini, 1 cookie, herb tea

Mid-afternoon snack: Rest of the package of cookies, 1 qt. ice cream, 1 jar hot fudge

Dinner: 2 loaves of garlic bread, large cheese and sausage pizza, a pitcher of root beer, 3 candy bars, entire cheesecake eaten directly from the fridge

Okay, that's not the best way to start or finish the day, but I can see many who will commit to this diet.

My mom tells the story of when she took me to a Boy Scout all-you-can-eat breakfast fundraiser. I had eaten 21 pancakes and several sausages and I could have kept going if Mom hadn't pushed me out the door. That's not what I had in mind when I say to eat a good breakfast. I am just a normal guy who likes a good breakfast. I think starting out the day with a good meal sharpens us mentally and delivers a sense of satisfaction, giving us the fuel to live positively more often and that is healthy.

 I find it of the utmost importance in my life to read the Bible and pray before I walk out the door. I consider this to be time communicating with God. For me, I spend this time in the morning. I know people work various shifts and need to have a different time scheduled. At one time, I worked rotating shifts and know that creates a unique schedule and rhythm. You could say reading my Bible is my spiritual meal. Time reading and praying nourishes a person spiritually. If you don't have a regular time to read the Bible, I want to encourage you to establish a time. You don't need to read much, but read enough that you can think about it. Then, spend some time and pray about the day ahead of you, for your loved ones, and just quiet yourself in God's presence. I consider this essential to positive living.

There are great benefits to living positively. Each step we take toward this mindset brings greater health. The Mayo Clinic staff put together an article I kept from one of my vacations to the Mayo Clinic. See, isn't that a positive way to look at my time at the hospital? I kept the following portion of the article that I find motivating entitled "The Health Benefits of Positive Thinking."

Researchers continue to explore the effects of positive thinking and optimism on health. Health benefits that positive thinking may provide include:

* Increased Life Span

* Lower rates of depression

* Lower rates of distress

* Greater resistance to the common cold

* Better psychological and physical well being

* Better cardiovascular health and reduced risk of death from cardiovascular disease

* Better coping skills during hardships and times of stress.[1]

The research is telling us to live the day positively. To experience these benefits, we need to start the day right.

7 Schedule Hobbies and Fun Outings

I stole this one from the Christian counselor I went to see several years ago. As he sat and listened to me share where I was at in my journey, I could see his brow wrinkle and I knew I was in the right place. He said to me, "Matt, what do you like to do for a hobby?" I thought, "I am here to get stuff figured out, not to discuss hobbies." He made me list what I would do if I had a day off and money was no obstacle. To me, the answer came quickly: play basketball somewhere, get together with some friends, maybe golf. I get energized coaching sports. I like watching football with my family. He then asked when was the last time that I had been involved in any of these activities. I remember, to my shock, I had hardly done any of those activities in several months and I realized that had contributed to my difficult times.

So I pass that on to you. If you and I want to live positively, we need room in our lives to engage in hobbies and activities that fill up our emotional tanks. For the past 20 years, Cyndy and I have gone with our friends John and Becky to the boys' state basketball tournament in Madison, Wisconsin. John and I spend a solid two days watching games, and Cyndy and Becky shop and hang out at the motel. They then join us for a couple of games on Friday morning. This trip never ceases to help fill up my tanks. I love basketball and even more, spending time with Cyndy and our dear friends.

Engage with the people and activities that help fill your emotional, relational, physical, and even spiritual tanks.

I want to close this chapter with this encouraging thought I found on Positive Outlooks Blog by Jay Danzie. Danzie writes,

"Your smile is your logo, your personality is your business card, how you leave others feeling after an experience with you becomes your trademark." [2]

Being your normal requires living positively, and when you and I do that, we have a great influence which is a trademark that we all aspire to leave.

CHAPTER SEVEN:
Live Authentically

*"Gardening forces you to be in the moment, to deal
with what is happening in the here and now. Plants
can't fake it like human beings can. They don't tell you
everything is fine if it isn't. That's why observation is
the single most useful talent to cultivate."* [1]

Authenticity means being genuine. Real. Being our normal is living a life free from false fronts.

To be who God created us to be requires that we stop trying to be who we were never created to be.

I have learned how easy it is to fake it. I've told others things are fine when deep down I was anything but fine. I have misrepresented the truth to protect my image. I have learned over the years that the mask-wearing game seems to offer benefits but only results in duplicity and loneliness. We miss out on opportunities to be understood and really known and loved for being our normal.

The major difficulty with inauthentic living is that it isn't real. Performance-based living may make a good impression, but behind the exterior person, there is little freedom or confidence. However, when we live with transparency, an honest realism develops. I know from experience that it is frightening to open up to others. I want to assure you that any risk you face is worth it. There is an assurance in living, which is rewarded only to those who live authentically.

It's being our normal that will allow us to really have a powerful influence. It's our normal that will bring the most peace and joy. The comparison trap will only lead you to unending dissatisfaction as you chase someone else's life. Our normal allows us to live free from assaulting guilt and the drudgery of a mediocre life. What a way to live!

The most powerful influence we can have comes when our journey rubs off on others and influences them to become their normal. The key point in that transaction is others' ability to understand and know us. If we don't provide opportunities for others to see our hearts, minds, priorities, and relationships, our normal remains hidden and a mystery to others. Thus, we limit how we can impact others' lives for the good.

Opening our lives to others is much like opening our homes. It is an invitation for others to come in, make themselves at home, and relate on personal levels. When someone comes into my home they see interactions, the contents of my bookshelves, pictures on the wall, and even the messiness along with all kinds of interesting things. This is what my friends Tom and Chris did years ago. I was a very young Christian and when I met Tom, we became fast friends. Tom had been a Christian for many years and really mentored me. He taught me how to study the Bible and how to lead groups. I think the greatest thing he did, though, was letting me see his life up close and personal. He invited me into his home. I watched how he interacted with Chris and the kids. He never tried to portray himself as having it all together.

When we played basketball together, which we did a lot, he would get frustrated at times and his competitiveness would get the best of him. He would apologize or confess it. He was the real deal. What a gift to me. Tom served as my best man, and his daughter Becky played piano at our wedding. Tom and his family stood with us as our first child Angela's support sponsors when we dedicated her. It was a no-brainer to choose him to speak at my ordination service. Although living in Utah at that time, Tom and Chris were gracious enough to fly to Wisconsin to speak and celebrate the occasion with us. They are truly special people to us. They have been great models of what it means to live an authentic life.

I believe authentic living and relationships are key to leading well. Our elder board meets twice a month. The first meeting of the month is held in one of our homes. There is something more intimate about meeting in a home. We want to seize opportunities to build our team as we move toward greater authenticity in our relationships.

Like opening our homes, when we open our lives we let others in to see the genuine person. Whatever God is doing, changing, and transforming in our lives then becomes a connecting point with others. When our normal is genuine, it has an influence on others.

Some years ago, I took part in an intensive leadership training. The seminar included trainers and coaches who were pretty hard-charging leaders. They presented very structured tips. They talked about leading with authority, adapting business models, and securing financial health within our organizations. They shared steps to building a winning team and advice on how to remove obstacles that were preventing the growth of the organizations we were leading. I remember working diligently to put together a very detailed plan, organizational structure, and tiered measurement systems that I would use to move the church where I pastored forward to greater success. But the principles merged too closely to the presenters' personalities. After some time, I found myself trying to be someone I was not. I began heading down a road that was taking me away from my normal. What God pointed out to me was that He created me, my temperament, and my personality. To have the impact I desired would require me to accept this and pursue my normal.

In his book, "Integrity", Henry Cloud points out the ingredients that are part of a true impact that flows from living authentically:

Research shows that models who are followed, which ultimately means trusted, are models who have the following characteristics:

1. They possess strength.

2. They possess "likeness" to the ones following them.

3. They are warm.

4. They are imperfect, and coping models, as opposed to the perfect ones. [2]

While there are common characteristics of having influence, these commonalities don't negate the variety of personalities and diversity of gifts we have.

God gave me the abilities He wanted me to have and develop. I am to align myself with who He wants me to be, not someone else's personality or passions. I look back now at that leadership training and shake my head at my immaturity and insecurity. The speakers and trainers weren't necessarily wrong, and it wasn't that they had misplaced priorities; in fact, they offered a lot of good ideas and principles. The problem was with me because I wrongly believed I needed to adopt their personalities, gifts, abilities, and perspectives to become successful. I learned a lot from that experience and I still need to take time evaluating when I read and go to conferences.

I have a dream to be a part of a church that demonstrates increasing transparency. Where people are quick to initiate conversations and willing to share their stories. A place where there are no pretenses or masks. Instead, there are stories shared of bankruptcies, unemployment, addictions and failed marriages, and how God transformed those people and their circumstances.

I know that the lack of transparency is an attempt to preserve our dignity, but what happens instead is it weakens our influence and our resolve. I think that is one reason the Old Testament Book of Psalms is so powerful. Psalms portrays people who have an honest faith, not a fake faith. Within the pages of Psalms, we find others with whom we can relate who wrestled with life and God.

The reason we can attract people when we are transparent is the same reason people like to read Psalms. They can relate to an honest and real faith even in the midst of life's upheavals.

What may be a surprise to those who know me well is there are times in my life I'd question if anyone liked being my friend or if they were just being nice. When I became a youth pastor and then a lead pastor, I thought, "Do these people really like me or do they socialize with me just because I am their pastor?" I didn't know how I was perceived and I probably cared too much what others thought. I finally came to a settled peace that I am pursuing my best normal and if others don't like that or if they don't "click" with me, that's okay.

The reality is that for you and me to have enriching relationships requires us to live aligned with who we are. If we don't, our relationships are based on a misrepresentation of who we are. I love and gravitate toward honest people—people who have no pretenses and are consistently the same person. I like it when I don't have to guess if what I see is really what a person is like or not.

That is one of many reasons I am in awe of the life Jesus lived when He walked this earth. People flocked to Jesus. They came from all around. They saw in Him one who was authentic, who loved them, who acted with kindness and humility. He extended grace and also spoke the truth at the same time. He was a magnet and a person who radically impacted people's lives. He still is and He still does!

If you or I have trouble admitting our shortcomings or areas where we are not strong, this should be a flag. If you have trouble telling people the truth about who you are and what you think, for one reason or another, that should be a flag. The flag being raised is telling you to step back and ask, "Is this the real me that others are seeing? If not, why not?" To live with confidence and impact others for the good comes from a life that is whole. There is not a private self and a public self. Rather, seek to cultivate an attitude that says, "I will open the door to my life and let others see my normal." If you are not normally self-disclosing, I encourage you to take small steps toward greater transparency. You will be surprised by the impact of those small steps. One discovery you'll make is how others will welcome your self-disclosure. Your normal and your willingness in allowing others to see into your life will result in an attractive and inviting lifestyle.

There may be times in your willingness to be honest about your life when someone might judge that as a weakness. Others' refusal to live authentically is a reflection on them. Focusing your energy on being genuine is not minimized by others' insecurities. Keep pursuing authentic living.

Over the years, Cyndy and I have hosted small groups in our homes. Our goal was to get to a place with those in the group where everyone felt comfortable, relaxed, and safe. To do that, we asked everyone to wear sweatpants or pajamas to our group meetings. Especially one group really bought into it. Whether it was Bob's flannel pants or Jon's full pajama set with slippers, we grew quite close as a group. Setting the tone by dressing down allowed the group to begin to let down their guard. Cyndy and I still have that goal for our small groups!

I have noticed that when I share some of my insecurities and doubts with other leaders they sit up and listen. It's not that they aren't engaged, but when I let them see into my life they can relate to that. Our transparency with others creates an atmosphere in which it is safe to talk about the doubts, the issues that plague us, and the hidden and unresolved issues that still hurt us. I have learned that my honesty elicits honesty among others, and it is honest, transparent discussion that allows any organization to flourish by building on strengths and identifying where there are weaknesses. When I interviewed to become the lead pastor with the church where Cyndy and I now serve, I remember sitting in one of the elder's living room with the search team and sharing some things that felt vulnerable. Afterward, I remember telling Cyndy something along the lines of, "I am not sure they will want me after what I shared." I am glad I did because I really wanted them to sense who I was, as choosing a pastor is a very important decision for a church.

If we are to live authentically we must, and I emphasize must, start with the source of the struggle. This might not be a news flash, but you and I are sinners. We have sinned against God by nature and choice. When I say we need to be authentic and real, I don't mean we overlook sin and just live carelessly. We can't be bursting out in anger, swearing up a storm, or slandering others and excusing it by saying, "Well, that is just who I am." That is dishonest at the deepest level and that will only create distance— distance from God, from others, and from you experiencing your normal.

To live authentically is to admit you are a sinner separated from God and not aligned with God or who He created you to be. A genuine person doesn't excuse sin but repents of it. He doesn't flaunt his sin or parade it around. He boasts in the grace of God, which brings freedom in living. The only reason I can even write about being authentic is because of God's grace in forgiving me, accepting me, and calling me His child. Living authentically, which is closely linked with integrity, must begin on the inside.

In the first book of the Bible, Genesis, we read that Adam and Eve had everything they could ever want and they had an intimate relationship with God. Believing a lie from Satan, they chose to disobey God and the struggle with living authentically began. We realize the result of their sin when we read, "Then the eyes of both of them were opened, and they realized they were naked; so they sewed fig leaves together and made coverings for themselves. Then the man and his wife heard the sound of the Lord God as he was walking in the garden in the cool of day, and they hid from the Lord among the trees of the garden. But the Lord God called to the man, 'where are you?' He answered, 'I heard you in the garden, and I was afraid because I was naked; so I hid'" (Genesis 3:7-10 NIV).

It is very instructive that after the man and woman sinned, they recognized they were naked; they tried to cover themselves and then they hid. It was at that moment that mankind began to struggle with what it means to be real and genuine. Sin causes us to hide—hide who we are and what we do. We are tempted to hide from God and from others. Instead of being open and vulnerable, many people choose to hide behind facades and inconsistencies. Sin will work against us in our efforts to align our lives with our normal.

When we choose to live and act in ways that are not consistent with who we are, we deceive ourselves. It will take humility to recognize this and intentionality to turn away from the inconsistencies and facades. Pride is offensive to God because it takes us from a position of cooperating with God and His plans for us to one of fighting both the plan and Maker.

King David prayed these words, "Lord, who may dwell in your sacred tent? Who may live on your holy mountain? The one whose walk is blameless, who does what is righteous, who speaks truth from His heart" (Psalm 15:1-2 NIV). The psalmist recognized that those who enjoy the rich blessing of God's presence are those who live a righteous life, those who are authentic in their hearts. When I am honest, I know that there are times when I desire to be exalted and I become alienated from those who do not affirm me. I must be honest and confess this if I want to walk in forgiveness, confidence, and freedom. I need to be real within myself, before God, and with others when needed, before I can hope to be real on the outside.

We allow shame, guilt, and anxiety in our lives when we are not honest with God and with ourselves. In Psalm 25:21, the writer of the Psalm, David, shares his desire, "May integrity and uprightness protect me, because my hope, Lord, is in you."

Authenticity protects you and me from living a life of lies. God rewards those who are honest and have a humble heart. Pursue living authentically and start on the inside, before God.

Living authentically is a celebration of your normal. Pursue consistent authenticity. It has taken me a long time to get comfortable in my normal, but I am in a much better place. When living with authenticity, I am driven by a passion for life and for others. When I live with a false front, I am left to the shallowness of performing. The following prayer reveals how transformation is at the core of moving to a deeper and genuine life.

O persistent God,
deliver me from assuming your mercy is gentle.
Pressure me that I may grow more human,
not through the lessening of my struggles,
but through an expansion of them. . .

Deepen my hurt until I learn to share it
and myself openly, and my needs honestly.
Sharpen my fears until I name themselves
and release the power I have locked in them
and they in me.
Accentuate my confusion
until I shed those grandiose expectations
that divert me from the small, glad gifts
of the now and the here and the me.
Expose my shame where it shivers,
crouched behind the curtains of propriety,
until I can laugh at last
through my common frailties and failures,
laugh my way toward becoming whole. [3]

The reward and influence are great when we persistently pursue an authentic life.

CHAPTER EIGHT:

Discern Your Unique Mission

It's in Christ that we find out who we are and what
we are living for. Long before we first heard of Christ and
got our hopes up, he had his eye on us, had designs on
us for glorious living, part of the overall purpose he is
working out in everything and everyone.

Ephesians 1:11-12 (MSG)

A life-changing truth that you and I must embrace is that there
is a unique calling on our lives. Once we believe that, we can
consider what that calling entails and what it looks like to live out
that calling. There are two fruitful efforts that I find incredibly
helpful to live out one's unique calling: pursuing self-awareness
and intentionally focusing on your spheres of influence.

Pursue Self-Awareness

I am convinced that there is a place in our lives, a sweet spot,
where we function at maximum capacity. What I mean, in a
more specific way, is that when we align our personality, abilities,
spiritual disciplines, personal mission, and opportunities, our
lives will influence others in great ways. The more we cultivate
each of these areas, the greater the basis we have to discover
what we are capable of accomplishing. It is important to believe
that God can use our lives to accomplish His purposes. Our

conviction about this enhances our sensitivity in recognizing the hand of God, breeding cooperation with what He is asking us to do.

We live in such a noisy world. Many are trying to tell us what to do. You know this because of all the infomercials and the onslaught of media opinions and promotions. I could flip through the channels and "discover" how to lose 10 pounds in one week, get ripped abs, improve my cardio, cook only organic, build a million-dollar business, flip houses, get rid of cellulite, improve my sex life, and more. A simple phrase that I often revisit is, "less confusion and more clarity."

Let me ask you a question. What do you feel is the mission of your life? Are you clear on it? Another way to ask the question is, "When you lie on your death bed, what will you regret not having done?" When I revisit the reality that I only have one shot at living this life, it pulls me up short. Every time!

We must live with a sense of urgency. There are no "do-overs" with regard to living our lives. We need to clarify our life's mission. Self-awareness can lead us to identify a personal mission that will give guidance to our priorities and activities. So how do we do that?

* Consider some of the critical people or occurrences in your life. Identify how they impacted you. Perhaps you can specifically record the imprint others have left on your life.

* Consider the painful experiences you have had and evaluate how they have helped to shape your life.

90

* Identify core convictions. These core convictions are the areas we would never fudge on. They are embedded within our hearts and spirit. [1]

For example, the highest priority in my life is to bring glory to God. Everything in my life is centered around that. This helps me focus on my day-to-day choices but also frees me from living to always please people. So, as I lie on my deathbed, I wouldn't be satisfied if I had tried to please everyone. I will be satisfied if I have sought out God's pleasure in all I have done with a dogged determination. I have a deep conviction that the most important question I need to ask every night as I lay my head on my pillow is, "Did I love well today? Did I love God well and did I love people well?" If I can say "yes", then I lived well that day.

Acting on a desire to live more intentionally, several years ago I spent time identifying my personal mission. This has been one of the most helpful exercises I have ever done. I keep a copy in my wallet and read it often. I crafted this statement after reflecting on the questions listed at the beginning of this chapter. I identified the events and the people who have impacted my life. I considered the painful experiences in my life and evaluated how they have contributed to who I am today. I identified what my core convictions (also called core values) are. You know they are the core when even other people can identify what you believe strongly. I share my mission with you so that you can get a glimpse of what it looks like to clarify your life's mission.

I also want to be clear that I have to grow in so many ways to see the fruits I'd like to see. This statement contains my convictions about what I am called by God to pursue in my life.

I live to bring glory to Almighty God by the worship of who He is, by an authentic faith and lifestyle that reflects God's grace and truth, and by giving of myself to His calling in my life. God has specifically called me:

* To my Savior and a growing intimacy with Him.

* To my wife Cyndy. To cherish her and serve her. To help her discover her giftedness, her role in ministry, and to build her up.

* To my children. To love them and train them to follow Jesus. To leave a legacy for them to live and pass on— a legacy marked by an active faith in Christ, prayer, compassion, integrity, and faithfulness.

* To my family and brothers and sisters in Christ. To model for them and encourage them in a deeper walk with Christ. To encourage them to give their lives for the kingdom of God by helping them discover their individual God-given gifts. To pray for and mentor a new generation of leaders.

* To my world. To pray for and expose others to the love, the life, and the hope that is found in Jesus Christ. My mission field begins at home and then extends to my neighbors, my community, and to the outermost parts of the world.

My mission statement allows me to maintain focus. It also allows me to focus my prayers and better encourage these people. The best change happens when we decide what will never change. I encourage you to spend time pursuing self-awareness and crystallizing your personal mission. I have become more excited and passionate about writing this book as I have realized this avenue is allowing me to live out my personal mission in one way.

In pursuing self-awareness, a laser-like focus develops that helps to simplify life. This focus results in deep influence. In the "Minute with Maxwell" video clip, John Maxwell said, "Awareness plus ability plus choices equals capacity" (July 6, 2018). What I think he is hitting on is that when we shift our focus from what we can't do to what we are able to do well, we begin to see new opportunities.

Self-awareness is an ongoing process. I began to put some pieces together in my early 20s. Growing up, I had always been the one in my neighborhood to take the lead in organizing games and rounding up guys to play ball. In high school, I seemed to always wind up as captain or leading practice if the coach stepped away. I didn't realize it then, but I naturally flowed into leadership roles. I wasn't afraid of it; it came easily for me. I have coached basketball, football, softball, and even volleyball. I love to coach. It energizes me. I have coached pastors over the years and I have pastored churches. No matter where I go in life, I flow into leadership roles. God has wired me that way. There is no other explanation. When we are self-aware, we can put pieces together and get a clearer look at our lives and our future. My leadership flows from my normal. If not, it is flawed leadership.

There is a subtle deception that creeps in when we believe that we must possess someone else's personality, gifts, temperament, or status in life before we can significantly impact others' lives. Don't believe that lie! God demonstrates His grace, wisdom, beauty, and mercy in His work in the lives of normal people. Your normal is extraordinary! This leads to the second intentional focus.

✡ Focus on Your Spheres of Influence

Faith focuses beyond the present, beyond "what is" to "what could be." And what "could be" is influencing lives in great ways in your spheres of influence. In my case, I am seeking to focus on my sphere of influence in my home, within the church, in my community, and beyond. You are the book others are reading and new pages are being added every day of your life. Be careful of what is contained in those pages. What do those in your home read? What about those who you work alongside? What do your neighbors see? What do those in the church see? We would be very wise to consider these questions and give attention to what makes up the contents of the pages of our days.

God has positioned you where you are in regard to relationships and your location. He has provided a platform for you to have great influence. Don't waste your opportunities.

It is summer as I write this, and I have chosen to umpire 12 and under girls' softball league games. I have decided to make it my goal to compliment and engage in conversation with as many of the girls and their parents as possible. It really seems the girls have responded. I umpired the same team from a neighboring town and the catcher said to me, "Oh good, you're umping again." I know she was simply saying, "I am glad to have the encouragement and fun again." That blessed my heart and caused me to thank God. He may be using my normal to shine for Him in this specific sphere of influence. Anyone umpiring could bring the same encouragement, eliciting the same response from that catcher. Once again, intentionality is needed.

Cyndy and I have been intentional in seizing opportunities that allow us to meet new people. The times I have coached a school athletic team, Cyndy came and watched the games. I would be trying to impact lives on the court at the same time she was trying to impact lives in the bleachers. We did that on purpose, and it allowed our normal to impact more lives. It is a great practice to plan for impacting lives.

My friends, Chad and Emily, hosted a Bible Study on marriage each week before volleyball league games. They would invite couples in their sphere of influence who liked to play volleyball and who wanted to invest in their marriage. Jon and Jamie decided to turn their yard into a campsite and invite families from their spheres of influence over for a weekend of fun and engagement. New friendships were forged and families got time away. Jordan and Sheila hosted card parties, which usually had between 12-16 players. They invited people from their spheres of influence. They went a step further and asked those who had children to bring them along. The older children watched the younger children, and there was fun for all and relationships being formed and strengthened. Each of these individuals didn't have to become great at anything or have a perfect gathering planned. They didn't need more money. They just did what they liked and what was natural to them and invited others to join in.

What are your hobbies and interests? Do you enjoy concerts or movies? Sporting events? Art? Whatever you enjoy and like to do naturally, invite someone you know to join.

Cyndy and I are hosting card parties. We have found that this is natural and enjoyable for us and it allows us to get to know others who God has brought into our sphere of influence. I am sure my friends I just mentioned would agree that it seems natural to reach out to others in the ways they have chosen.

Why not, each morning, identify who you will encounter that day and ask God to help you in a specific way to encourage them. God loves that prayer and will also allow us to see what opportunities there are to bring that encouragement to others. Also, remind yourself to have your antennae up when you are in grocery stores, waiting rooms, and at school functions. The normal you has a calling on your life and now is the time to identify and pursue that calling.

CHAPTER NINE:
Discover the Power of Words

A good person produces good things from the treasury
of a good heart, and an evil person produces evil things
from the treasury of an evil heart. What you say
flows from what is in your heart.

Luke 6:45 (NLT)

Note: I would like to encourage you to consider reading this chapter out loud to your family and/or roommates. It is that important.

What does our speech have to do with living a normal life? Sure, it's important, but really—a whole chapter dedicated to our speech? According to Jesus, our words reflect the condition of our hearts. We were created to communicate in ways that encourage others to be who God created them to be. There is power in our words. Every person reading this has been created in such a way that words bring clarity to the condition of our alignment with our normal.

When we look all around God's creation, we see that only human beings have the ability to communicate through the spoken word. The ability to use words is a unique and powerful gift from God. The Bible shows us, again and again, a connection between our hearts and our mouths. I think that many miss this connection. When we pursue our normal, we must pay attention to our words for they reveal what is going on inside ourselves. Our words not only reveal what's in the heart, but our words also affirm the authenticity of our pursuit of our normal. If we are serious about becoming who God wants us to be, we won't want to ignore this area of our lives. The writer of Proverbs tells us, "The tongue has the power of life and death, and those who love it will eat its fruit" (Proverbs 18:21 ESV).

Words are not simply sounds caused by air passing through our larynx. Words do more than convey information. Words can destroy one's spirit and even stir up hatred and violence. They can inflict wounds or worsen them. Make no mistake—words have power!

In light of the power of words, a key question for every one of us is: "Are we using words to build up people or bring harm to them?" Are our words filled with hate or love, bitterness or blessing, complaining or compliments?

I have done a fair amount of pre-marital counseling for couples over the years. Time and time again, I have seen couples amazed at the amount of Bible passages that speak to what and how we communicate. Here are a few.

"The mouth of the righteous produces wisdom,
but a perverse tongue will be cut out. The lips of the
righteous know what is appropriate, but the mouth
of the wicked, only what is perverse."

Proverbs 10:31-32 (ESV)

"A gentle answer turns away anger, but a harsh word
stirs up wrath. The tongue of the wise makes knowledge

attractive, but the mouths of fools blurt out foolishness. . .
The tongue that heals is a tree of life, but a devious
tongue breaks the spirit."

Proverbs 15:1-2,4 (ESV)

"A word spoken at the right time is like gold
apples in silver settings."

Proverbs 25:11 (ESV)

"A bit in the mouth of a horse controls the whole horse.
A small rudder on a huge ship in the hands of a skilled
captain sets a course in the face of the strongest winds.
A word out of your mouth may seem of no account,
but it can accomplish nearly anything—or destroy it!

It only takes a spark, remember, to set off a forest fire.
A careless or wrongly placed word out of your mouth
can do that. By our speech we can ruin the world, turn
harmony to chaos, throw mud on a reputation, send the
whole world up in smoke and go up in smoke with it,
smoke right from the pit of hell.

This is scary: You can tame a tiger, but you can't tame
a tongue—it's never been done. The tongue runs wild,
a wanton killer. With our tongues we bless God our Father;
with the same tongues we curse the very men and women
He made in His image. Curses and blessings out of
the same mouth!"

James 3:3-10 (MSG)

These few verses make it quite clear that God cares about how we communicate. The above Scripture affirms that we have a choice of how we will speak and that there are consequences for what we say. Jesus added even more weight to the seriousness of how we speak when He said, "But I tell you that every careless word that people speak, they shall give an accounting for it in the Day of Judgment" (Matthew 12:39 NASB).

Our speech is a serious issue. We will be held accountable for how we speak. We must consider this when we evaluate our normal. When we are aligned with our normal, we will bless and not curse. We will encourage and not tear down.

Robert Wolgemuth, in his excellent book "The Most Important Place on Earth" says, "Mouths are loaded guns, and words they speak can be lethal. . . When words are spoken, they're always real. Words are never blanks. They're actual bullets, and their impact is absolute. Every time." [1] It is helpful and challenging to look at our speech as a loaded gun and our words as bullets. When we do, it causes us to evaluate the harm that results from careless words. Words are never blanks; they are always real. They have an impact every time.

I try to use my words carefully, but I realize that I have hurt people with my words. The hard reality is that you and I can't take them back. In his book, Woglemuth uses an expression, "words need to be carried about with utmost care." That phrase resonates with me. I don't want to hurt others with my words, and the times I have, it is because I did not use my words with care. What a very practical, but essential area of our lives to evaluate and address. No wonder the psalmist prayed, "Set a guard over my mouth, O Lord; Keep watch over the door of my lips" (Psalm 141:3 NIV).

I, unfortunately, have several journal entries that testify to carelessness in my words and the grief that I carried over the damage they caused. One such time, years ago, I was a coach on the staff of a high school girls' softball team. We were playing in an important tournament game and if we won, we had a great shot of winning the state tournament. We were down by a couple of runs late in the game. We had a runner on second and the next batter hit a hard, base hit to the outfield. Our runner on second tried to score and was thrown out at home. After the game as the coaches were talking, one of us made a comment about the mistake the player made. I mentioned something along the lines of how that play probably cost us the game. I didn't know it, but that girl and her teammate were standing behind me, within earshot. The following week, the girl's mom contacted me to let me know that her daughter had overheard what I said and was hurt. This young lady was incredibly mature and fun-loving; she possessed a strong character. I knew I needed to apologize and she was gracious to forgive me. The hardest hit that day had not been the ball, but a person and I had struck her with my words. I cringe just writing about it.

Along with hurting others personally, our words can also hurt our reputation as well as our capacity to build trust with others. We are all a part of a network of relationships and what undergirds the strength of those relationships is trust. There is a principle, for Christians especially, related to our words that we are often unaware of. If we violate integrity through our words in more casual moments, then we undermine the capacity of our words to carry appropriate validity when we speak as a follower of Jesus. If we talk about our love for God, but we are also speaking unloving and untrue words to others, there is a disconnect that is confusing to others trying to find their way on their spiritual journey. That is why we must consistently pay attention to cultivate a disciplined tongue.

In the realm of leadership, I have experienced and observed that fewer things erode respect, trust, and admiration more than a consistent pattern of misspoken and inappropriate words. I can think of meetings where I wrote "watch your words" at the top of my meeting agenda because going in, I knew there were topics that would be discussed in which I held firm convictions. I knew I would be tempted to speak forcibly so I could win others to my side. I knew if I didn't set a reminder in place to listen first and then speak in ways that foster unity and agreement, then I would be acting outside of God's will. I can think of times that I was probably right in a decision but wrong in how I communicated it. Too many nights I have laid in bed repenting because I did not love others well enough, as evidenced by the carnage my words left behind.

My youngest daughter is in high school and she shares with me how mean-spirited some of her classmates can be in the use of their words. I grieve when I hear that because I know the power of words and the hurt that is being experienced by many teenagers at such a difficult time in their lives. She shares with me, and it's easy to see, all the harmful ways people use words on social media. I am very proud of how careful my daughter is with her words.

I have really cut down on how often I message people through texting and Facebook. I don't want to drift into impersonal communication and risk saying foolish things or have something taken out of context. We all can testify how easy it is to focus on what not to say, but I feel we would better served to focus more on what to say.

Develop words and phrases that clearly communicate positive encouragement; use statements that communicate value to people.

Begin to use them. Phrases as simple as, "You're awesome" carry a lot of impact. I use the phrase, "That is kind of you" to let others know I recognize their efforts. Be intentional! Let's learn to freely use "bullets" that have a positive impact. We give others a gift when we speak words that are tender, gracious, encouraging, and truthful.

I can think of several people who have given me the gift of gracious, healing, and hope-filled letters. We have dear friends, Hilmer and Bonnie, who whenever we see them, have never failed to bless us with words of affirmation. They have sent us numerous letters over the years that have brought me to tears with the hope they held. They have reminded me over and over that God could use me in even greater ways. I keep them and have needed them many times over the years in my pastoral ministry. I have a letter from a friend Andrea who participated in the youth group I led. She shared how God has used me in her life. I kept it and find great motivation in re-reading the letter.

Now, I have also received comments, letters, and emails that communicate how poorly I was doing things or how someone disagreed with a decision I made. I learn what I can, but then I throw them out. I know far worse things about myself than what anyone else could write. It is important that we work hard to not speak in unhealthy ways that are often culturally accepted such as gossip and slander. Written on a notecard that I view periodically, I have three guiding principles that relate to what I will communicate. I ask myself:

#1 – Is it true?
#2 – Is it confidential?
#3 – Is it helpful?

Those three evaluating questions are helpful in guarding my speech. They will also help you. The bottom line is that we have a choice to build up or tear down with our words. If you want to live and grow in being your normal, then steward your words with care.

CHAPTER TEN:
Develop Sheltering Friendships

God has given me some incredible friends. By "friends", I don't mean just acquaintances or surface relationships. Friends do come in varying degrees. Some play more significant roles in our lives. We have acquaintances, casual friends, and a few close friends. Acquaintances and casual friends usually bring limited contact and some common interests. We enjoy periodic time together and there is mutual benefit from these friendships. These are a blessing without a doubt.

When I use the word "friend", in a deeper sense than the average person might. I refer to a "close friend" as someone you can be vulnerable before, have regular contact with, and with whom you share a deeper commitment.

Within the last four years, I have faced a battle with colorectal cancer. Surgery was needed and it was successful at first but then the cancer metastasized (moved to) to my lung, which resulted in the doctors having to remove most of my left lung during a second surgery. It was a very difficult time for my whole family. What does stand out, looking back, is the support we received from our families and friends. I have a friend Jordan who traveled a total of nine hours to come to see me for an hour and a half after the first surgery. Not to be outdone, Jordan's wife, Sheila, came to sit with Cyndy and me before and through the second surgery. You know who your good friends are by who you allow to see you in your hospital gown. Sorry, Sheila.

Cyndy and I have some dear friends who I mentioned earlier, John and Becky, who traveled to Rochester, Minnesota, and stayed over at a motel the night they released us from the hospital just to be with us so we wouldn't feel alone in the battle. Our friends' actions communicated to Cyndy and I that we were loved and not alone. Their presence brings us comfort and shelter from the icy winds of fear, loneliness, and doubt. They model so well what I call sheltering friends. I get the word sheltering from a quote by Samuel Taylor Coleridge who once described friendship as "a sheltering tree." I find it a beautiful description. When the storms hit, friends don't pack up and leave. They stand firmly alongside you and protect you in prayer and with encouragement.

Laughter is a big part of my friendships. When I was diagnosed with colorectal cancer, it became clear I needed surgery to remove the tumor; it was not clear whether they could save the sphincter muscle. (Note: Now, at this point, I am hesitant to provide any more information. I will say it is a muscle in your rear end. If you're not up to date on your knowledge of the sphincter muscle, I suggest turning to another resource.) Having said that, my friend Jordan, especially, had a lot of fun talking about the radiation to my rear end and the surgery. We concluded that we should get t-shirts made that said, "Save the Sphincter" but then we thought maybe they wouldn't be appreciated, except by us. Between Jordan and my sister Mary, I discovered there are a lot of cards with butt jokes on them. Who knew? Oh, the joy, comfort, and support from sheltering friends.

You might be surprised to know that the words "friend", "friendly", and "friendship" appear over one hundred times in the

106

Bible. God says a lot about friendship. As I have read over these verses, I have found several truths about and characteristics of a close friendship—sheltering friendship.

I came across this one man's journal, and as I read through it, I found out he had experienced unparalleled fame, success, status, and influence. He had immeasurable wealth and had experienced many of the pleasures of the world. His journal reflects the regrets and lessons his experiences had taught him. The man is Solomon and the journal is the book of the Bible called Ecclesiastes. Solomon, the son of King David, inherited the throne and was blessed with great wisdom and wealth. This is the author of the Book of Ecclesiastes. In his journal, we read this:

> *There was a man all alone; he had neither son nor brother. There was no end to his toil, yet his eyes were not content with his wealth. "For whom am I toiling," he asked, "and why am I depriving myself of enjoyment?" This too is meaningless—a miserable business! Two are better than one, because they have a good return for their labor: If either of them falls down, one can help the other up. But pity anyone who falls and has no one to help them up. Also, if two lie down together, they will keep warm. But how can one keep warm alone? Though one may be overpowered, two can defend themselves. A cord of three strands is not quickly broken* (Ecclesiastes 4:8-12 NIV).

Solomon was in a sea of people but had no close friends. He even wondered why he was depriving himself of the enjoyment of friends. So, take it from someone who knew, two are better than one. Simply put, close friends empower you to be a better person.

107

Do you have close friends? When discussions about close friends take place, some conclude that it is more of a need for women. Yet numerous studies indicate this is not the case. Most men have many acquaintances, but very few men have a close friend. According to statistics, the average man over 35 years old does not have one close friend. The more time I spend time with people, the more convinced I am that men and women need to be taught how to develop and strengthen friendships. I am confident that Solomon also needed this kind of teaching. Solomon's words in Ecclesiastes reveal that he hadn't invested in friendships. The words written in Ecclesiastes teach truths about friendship that we would be wise to believe and to apply in our own lives.

One truth is that friends are not optional when it comes to life. They are essential. As Solomon says, ". . . pity the man who falls and has no one to help him up." There is no substitute for a friend—someone who cares, listens, laughs, empathizes, comforts, and if necessary, reproves. Friends are a gift from God.

I know my wife Cyndy would affirm the value of friends but I think she would stand on the conviction there is nothing better than a friend unless it's a friend who has chocolate. It is a wise woman I married.

Take it from Solomon, a closed-off life is a lonely and desperate life. The Ecclesiastes 4 passage also teaches that friendships don't come automatically. We must invest time and effort into building them. I have said it many times to my children and others, "If you want a friend, be a friend." It's not automatic. Knowing a person for twenty years doesn't make that person a close friend. It is not about duration. It's about what I addressed earlier, vulnerability.

I have a friend from Wisconsin: Eric. After meeting a couple of times, we began to be honest and vulnerable. As we discovered more about each other's lives and all our similarities, we were building a close friendship. It took time and willingness on both our parts. The blessing was well worth it as was the risk I took in letting my guard down. When he reads this, I guarantee Eric will make a sarcastic remark. We joke that is one of his spiritual gifts.

I believe the verses from Ecclesiastes and experience teach that friends are not neutral; they impact our lives. This is why it is crucial that we choose good friends—friends who will help us become our normal. If your close friends pursue living good lives and encourage you to be a better person, you're more likely to share a similar direction. However, the opposite is also true. If your close friends live careless and unproductive lives, they can lead you down the same path or worse. A verse from a New Testament book says, "Be not deceived; Bad company corrupts good morals" (1 Corinthians 15:33 NIV). So choose good company and close friends wisely. Friends will either help you or hurt you—they will impact you so choose close friends wisely if you want to live a life aligned with your normal.

When I think of my close friends, without exception I can think of ways they have helped me become a better person. There is something about a close friend that causes our hearts to be knit together. To use an older phrase, a friend is a kindred spirit.

Cyndy, the kids, and I have moved to three different communities and I have found in each place that God has provided a new, close friend. The current community we live in is unique in that there are many people who are content with superficial relationships.

When the storms of conflict or disagreements come, their relationships do not have sufficient depth to withstand the tension.

Being a pastor, I face a unique situation. After all, who wants to be the friend of the pastor? It is hard to find someone who can view me as Matt who happens to also be a pastor. For many, it's Pastor Matt and there is always a line that is hard for some to move beyond, to the point where they can relax and just share life as one person with another. No titles or agendas: just sharing lives. I have had a friendship weaken as the person began to approach our time together as a chance to influence me, trying to sway the pastor's mind on some church issues. I felt used, and when that happens, you don't feel safe. I am so grateful that God has brought a man into my life, Brett, with whom I am enjoying building a deeper friendship. Without his and his wife Sarah's belief in me and my message, it is doubtful that this book would have ever been published.

There was a ride at Great America in Illinois called the Giant Drop. Individuals would get strapped into a seat that would then be raised to a ridiculous height before stopping. Looking out for miles and seeing well beyond the park, those on this ride sat there until, all of a sudden, the chair dropped. Early in the day when our group walked by, I just watched the people getting off this ride. Some looked like they were going to have a heart attack, while others were greeting their friends who had waited at the bottom. There were high fives and hugs from those who waited at the bottom celebrating their survival. Then I went on the Giant Drop. I was grateful for the friends at the bottom but even more so for the friend who went on the ride with me. I had someone with whom to share the fear and the thrill. That's what close friends do. The crowd will wait at the bottom when your life hits up against hardships. A close friend will journey alongside you, providing support and a refuge when fear assaults. Invest in some sheltering friendships and you'll receive the benefits of their strength and insight.

When I was in my mid-twenties, I lived and worked in southern Wisconsin. I was at a very low point in my life. I was confused about what God wanted me to do. I felt alone and discouraged. I was downstairs helping my dad when I heard a voice call out. It was not just any voice. The voice of my close friend Tom brought instant comfort to me. We talked for two hours. Nothing had changed in my circumstances, yet after our conversation, it seemed it was all going to be okay. I didn't feel like such a failure because my friend brought me shelter in our friendship.

I would like to encourage you to take the following concrete steps to build and affirm your close friendships.

1. Tell your friends how you appreciate them through words or writing. Why don't you do that this week? I double dog dare you!

2. Plan a get together soon with a close friend or if you find you don't have any real close friends, start with someone you respect a lot and ask to meet with them more regularly. I know it will appear risky, but you will be surprised how many other people are also looking for close friends. Go ahead; take the step.

3. Pray with your friends—they and you need it. Prayer deepens any relationship.

CHAPTER ELEVEN:

Trust God

"Jesus supplies what we need in the moment, for the day,
for the season. And then He provides another grace after
that and another grace after that. Grace isn't a one-time
deposit. It's a moment-by-moment relationship with God,
where we trust Jesus to be in us and through us and for us.
We trust that he will come through in His own time and
in His own way. When we have no comeback,
the comeback is that Jesus is enough." [1]

-Louie Giglio

To live our normal requires us to trust God to peel away anything that is not of Him. Throughout this book, I have encouraged you to take steps and make applications. The degree to which you take those steps is tied to your trust in God. The decision comes down to whether you and I can trust that God will work in and through us as we take those steps. I have come to the conclusion that many people believe in a God they don't trust. We can believe Jesus died, rose again for our forgiveness, and that He can take us to heaven, but we still really struggle to trust Him in the day-to-day. In the midst of all the financial pressures, stresses of marriage, uncertain futures and our children's lives, we can be hesitant to trust God. In the New Testament book of Matthew, we read where Jesus strongly affirmed a childlike faith. "At that time the disciples came to Jesus, saying, 'Who is the greatest in the kingdom of heaven?' And calling to him a child, he put him in the midst of them and said, 'Truly, I say to you, unless you turn and become like children, you will never enter the kingdom of heaven. Whoever humbles himself like this child is the greatest in the kingdom of heaven'" (Matthew 18:1-4 ESV).

A childlike faith is a trusting faith. When my children were smaller, we would take long walks and there would come a point when they became tired and they would turn, raising their hands up to me. They would say, "Daddy carry me." They never questioned my strength, compassion, wisdom, or ability. They completely trusted me to carry them home.

There is so much for us to learn about living with a childlike faith and trust. Oswald Chambers once wrote, "The child-heart is open to any and all avenues; an angel would no more surprise it than a man. In dreams, in visions, in visible and invisible ways, God can talk and reveal Himself to a child; but this profound yet simple way is lost forever immediately when we lose the open, childlike nature." [2]

Why is it so hard to live a life of trusting God? For one, we have a misconception of what a life of faith and trust in God looks like. Trusting God does not mean there are no struggles or times when we blow it. As we read in the Bible, Abraham lied to save his own bacon. Moses has a bad temper and self-confidence issues. David committed adultery and battled depression. Solomon compromised his integrity. Job wrestled with God's sovereignty. Peter denied Jesus. These men are spiritual giants yet they failed miserably. In each of the above situations, these men's mistakes were followed by genuine repentance, and they continued to move forward.

This is the distinction between trusting God or not. All people will fail at times. But when the person who does not trust God fails, they wither under the failure. Those who trust God refuse to stay down. They believe God's promises and struggle back to their feet. By the power of the Holy Spirit, they keep moving forward. It may be a limp or seem like a crawl, but a deep, abiding trust propels them forward. They refuse to quit because they know God hasn't given up on them and He will carry them.

All through the Bible, we read accounts of people who struggled to trust God. So the challenge is not unique to us. There are many factors of why it's hard to trust God. Three emerge in my mind.

* We like to be in control.
* We think we have it under control.
* We may think God is not interested in our little world.

When we face some of the heart-wrenching challenges, we may even wonder if God is surprised or even knows what He is doing. We question whether God cares and if He can do anything about our situations. We would never say those thoughts out loud, but at the core of these thoughts exists the issue of whether we will trust God.

 I remember when Benjamin was born. We were hit in the gut with the suddenness and seriousness of his heart condition—pulmonary atresia. On Wednesday, August 9, 2000, Benjamin had his heart surgery. Here is what I entered in my journal. "Well, today is the surgery. We will know if Benjamin lives or dies from this surgery. I got to look in his eyes yesterday—what beautiful eyes. I want to be able to let out this huge breath and let out a scream of relief, but I don't yet feel I can. Forgive me,

114

Lord, if that is because of a lack of faith. This I know—You are good and merciful. I trust You." I remember and my journal reflects the wrestling of intentionally trusting God and not living in the grip of doubt. There is a great verse in the New Testament book of Hebrews: "Without faith it is impossible to please God because anyone who comes to Him must believe that He exists and rewards those who earnestly seek Him" (Hebrews 11:6 NIV). Faith that is active seeks after more of Him. When we earnestly seek Him, we are exercising trust. We are believing that the trip toward God will be worth it. God rewards those who exercise faith and trust. Sometimes that faith seems like a mustard seed (see Matthew 17:14-20; Luke 17:6). [3]

In these verses, Jesus uses a mustard seed as a visual lesson. By using the uncommonly small mustard seed as an example, Jesus is speaking figuratively about the incalculable power of God when unleashed in the lives of those with true faith. Biblical trust lies not in our ability but in God's character.

While in the waiting room in 2015, one of the doctors came back and said, "I am sorry to tell you we found a tumor. We need to do surgery." I remember a peace and a thought settled over me. The thought that surfaced was that God had me safely in His hands and there existed no place safer. The peace was the peace of God. There was no human reason to be at peace or to have the confidence I did.

As the chemo and radiation treatments progressed, I remember a question would periodically pop up: "Why was this happening?" The surgery was successful, and thankfully the surgeon saved the sphincter muscle! For several months following the surgery, I would wear a colostomy bag. (The bag collects your waste,

115

allowing the colon and rectum to heal.) I felt so beaten down and humiliated. I worked hard to hide my frustrations.

After my colon was sewn back together (colon resection) and the colostomy bag removed, I thought it would be back to normal function. Wow, was I wrong! My system has not worked right since, which has made me both humble and frustrated. Again, below the surface lurked the question: why?

Then, at a follow-up appointment two years later, my oncologist broke the news that my cancer had metastasized (spread) to my left lung, which would require surgery as soon as possible. I would lose most of my left lung. The question of "why was this happening" came more frequently. I trusted God but couldn't figure out the whole picture. Worse yet, I couldn't protect anyone from fear. The reality inside, where only God could see, was a struggle to trust anyone with what I felt. I wanted to protect Cyndy, the kids, the church where I pastor, as well as my family from worry and concern. It seemed like I was doing the right thing by holding back in sharing some of the battle. I had to force myself to share my fears. I was concerned I would increase people's anxiety. I am an optimistic person, which led me to be unfazed to a degree by the return of the cancer, but down deep I knew this was serious.

Then, the questions intensified. What will Cyndy do if I don't survive this surgery? What will happen if the cancer spreads even more? Will I get to see Benjamin and David graduate? Will I get to walk Angela and Emily down the aisle on their wedding days? Who will care for them? Those are hard and emotional questions I began to ask. I knew, when all was stripped away, it was a question of whether I would trust God with my family and my future. This is still the question. And it is your question. We need to decide if God is reliable and wise enough to be trusted. My only conclusion is a resounding yes. My assurance comes when I remember all the ways He has worked in my life in the past and His presence in my life today. I know He is unchanging and faithful in caring for His children.

I could write more about the challenge of trusting God, but I am saving that for the next book. To align my life with who I am created to be, I must trust God. When my daughter Angela was little, we bought a swing set. The box contained a trillion pieces—well, not that many but it sure seemed like it. We were in the garage putting it together. Angela had no idea what we were building. To her, it was just a bunch of pieces. Her attention was diverted from what we were doing. There came a point during the day, yes, it took us the whole day, where she recognized what we were building. She dropped what she was doing when she saw some of the magnificence of what we had built. She believed that I would finish it, and there would be a wonderful swing set that would fully satisfy her.

In the same way, I know that God is building something far greater than I can see in my life. He is in your life also. We may only see the pieces and it may not make any sense why those pieces are there, but we can trust that He is building and doing something magnificent. We are His handiwork, His design. That's the testimony of the Bible. "For we are God's handiwork, created in Christ Jesus to do good works, which God prepared in advance for us to do" (Ephesians 2:10 NIV).

This book itself came about because of Angela's encouragement. Looking back at an earlier statement that my daughter Emily made had me wondering if she had become a prophet. Cyndy and I had professional pictures taken when we were on a cruise. The

When?

package included individual poses as well. When Emily saw my picture, she said, "Dad, you look like an author." I did not grasp the pieces of my life and how God could bring them together to create a book in which I could share this message. I see God doing something that I never would have dreamed.

This moment you might find yourself standing at a fork in the road. One path is marked "business as usual." On this path, you keep doing what you've been doing before. It seems clearly laid out. However, it leads to a passionless and heartless place. A place with no peace. No hope.

There is another path marked "trust God." At first, this path seems narrow and uninviting. There are costs associated with this path. It requires humility, confession, and life alterations. This path leads to a bigger heart, a more passionate and authentic life. It leads to an extraordinary impact. Which path will you take?

From what I shared in this book, I believe God will help you discover who you are. I trust that He will communicate to you, the reader, that He has a plan for your life and that He wants to use the normal you to impact those in your sphere of relationships. I hope you trust Him to do so.

CHAPTER TWELVE:

Moving Forward Aligned

*"Above and around us God directs a grander saga,
written by His hand, orchestrated by His will, unveiled
according to His calendar. And you are part of it."* [1]

-Max Lucado

In God's story, normal matters. Normal men and women become
conduits of Divine activity. Yes, God has a part for you to play in
what He is doing around you. That is your extraordinary impact
and influence. It all begins with discovering your normal. In the
previous chapters, I have laid out specific ways you can discover
who God created you to be and how to live in alignment with
your authentic you. It bears repeating that our sin is a barrier
to not only knowing God personally but also to living out our
normal. It is only in trusting Jesus Christ as Savior that we find
the forgiveness and transforming power we need. (See Appendix
A on how to begin a relationship with God.) We can be sure
Jesus will always lead us toward greater alignment with who
He created us to be.

Years ago, Cyndy became very sick. She had become incredibly
weak and lost a lot of weight; she was dizzy and had no appetite.
Her chest felt heavy. She carried the frustration that she had little
energy to invest in our family. She suffered miserably for months.
After several visits to multiple doctors, an array of tests, no
diagnosis or relief were given. It was hard to watch. I felt helpless.

A friend suggested she expand her care to include a chiropractor. We were skeptical but desperate. Neither one of us had ever gone to a chiropractor. After her first visit, the initial adjustment brought instant relief. She said it actually felt like a miracle. The chiropractor shared that her back and neck were so far out of alignment that it was putting stress on the rest of her body. After she continued a couple more treatments, her body became fully aligned, providing amazing relief. She had freedom of movement, health, and energy to invest in our families' lives in a greater way. After all of the doctors' tests and efforts, it took an alignment to gain health. Cyndy paid a great price for being out of alignment. Likewise, there is a cost to leaving your life out of alignment. You will be left with stress in many areas of your life. There will be little freedom or confidence. Performance will become your default behavior. When out of alignment, we become unhealthy emotionally, relationally, and spiritually. We leave little in the way of impacting others in their journey.

This is why the issues this book addresses are so important. The degree to which we align our lives with our normal is the degree to which we will have an impact on others' lives. When we align our speech, we build others up, resulting in an extraordinary influence. When we recognize the value of people and our family and align our lives so as to demonstrate that we value them, we have an extraordinary impact that even extends into future generations. When we align our lives with an attitude that is positive, we affect the whole atmosphere of where we live, work, and socialize. When we live authentically, we cast aside the wasted energy and time of trying to perform. We are best able to glorify God with an honest heart.

When we realize our personal mission, it brings the drive of living and power to our influence. When we are intentional in building close friendships, we experience the joy and necessary support to journey together. When we trust God, we experience His grace in providing us with a new start, along with the power to persevere.

I hope you see the connection. When aligned with your normal, the places you traffic in become alive. Your home is warm and connected because you are there. Your workplace is better because your normal is there. Your marriage is stronger because of your normal. There is no area of your life unaffected by your influence. It begins with discovering your normal, and when we are in alignment with it, our influence extends and deepens.

The process of being increasingly aligned is a satisfying experience. In my experience of growing in consistency of alignment, I have discovered a correlating freedom, confidence, growth, and focus. The greater the alignment, the greater the passion, the greater the impact.

It's true; your normal is extraordinary!

A Prayer for My Readers

Dear Jesus,

I thank You for each person who is reading this. I ask that You would draw them to Yourself. Help each person to discover who they are in You and to experience the freedom and confidence in walking with You. Please take each hand and lead them to a greater love for You and for others around them. Might each life be lived for the praise of Your name. In Your name, Jesus, I pray.

Appendix A

How to Begin a Relationship With God

You need to believe:

1) God loves you and wants to give you peace, eternal life, and abundant life.

"For God so loved the world that he gave his one and only Son, that whoever believes in him shall not perish but have eternal life."

John 3:16 (NIV)

"Therefore, since we have been justified through faith, we have peace with God through our Lord Jesus Christ. . ."

Romans 5:1

2) You are sinful and separated from God.

"For the wages of sin is death, but the gift of God is eternal life in Christ Jesus our Lord."

Romans 6:23 (NIV)

". . . for all have sinned and fall short of the glory of God. . ."

Romans 3:23 (NIV)

3) Jesus paid the penalty for your sin when He died on the cross.

"Jesus answered, "I am the way and the truth and the life. No one comes to the Father except through me."

John 14:6

"But God demonstrates his own love for us in this: While we were still sinners, Christ died for us."

Romans 5:8

4) You must confess your sin and receive Jesus Christ as your Savior and Lord.

"Yet to all who did receive him, to those who believed in his name, he gave the right to become children of God."

John 1:12

"If we confess our sins, he is faithful and just and will forgive us our sins and purify us from all unrighteousness."

1 John 1:9

You must make a decision:

You can confess your sin and express your desire to be forgiven in prayer. Prayer is just talking to God. If your desire is to trust Jesus Christ as your Savior, make the following your prayer:

"Dear God, I believe You are Holy and that I'm a sinner. I confess my sin has separated me from You and I ask for Your forgiveness. I believe Jesus Christ is Your Son. I believe that He died for my sin and that You raised Him to life. I want to trust Him as my Savior and follow Him as Lord, from this day forward. Guide my life and help me to do Your will. I pray this in the name of Jesus. Amen."

Please email me and let me know if you made a decision to trust Jesus Christ or if I can help you in any way.

matt@mattnormalguy.com

Inspired by what you just read? Looking for a speaker for your next event?

Visit my website: mattnormalguy.com

References

Chapter 1

1. Merriam-Webster Online Dictionary

Chapter 2

1. Heschel, Abraham Joshua. *Man Is Not Alone: A Philosophy of Religion*. Farrar, Strauss & Giroux, 1951, page 227. As quoted in Gire, Ken. *The Reflective Life*. Chariot Victor Publishing,1998. Page 15.

Chapter 3

1. Brown, Brené. *The Hustle For Worthiness: Exploring the Power of Love, Belonging and Being Enough*. As quoted in Gire, Ken. *Relentless Pursuit*. Bethany House, 2012. Page 61.

2. Sam Speron, MD.

3. Heschel, Abraham Joshua. *God in Search of Man: A Philosophy of Judaism*. Farrar, Strauss & Giroux, 1955. Page 74.

Chapter 4

1. Planet, Paul. "Hugging Is an Excellent Source of Free Dopamine." The Dopamine Project Newsletter. July 11, 2011.

Chapter 5

1. Whitbourne, Susan Krauss. "What your Most Vivid Memories say About you" in *Psychology Today*. Nov. 20, 2012.

2. Ackerman, Diane. *A Natural History of the Senses*. Vintage, 1991.

Chapter 6

1. Mayo Clinic Staff. Rochester, Minnesota. Cancer Resource Center Pamphlet.

2. Danzie, Jay. *Positive Outlook Blog.*

Chapter 7

1. Handelsman, Judith. *Growing Myself: A Spiritual Journey Through Gardening.* Dutton, 1996. Page 129-130.

2. Cloud, Dr. Henry. *Integrity.* Harper Collins, 2006. Page 92.

3. Loder, Ted. *Guerillas of Grace.* Innisfree Press. 1984.

Chapter 8

1. Walling, Terry. *ChurchSmart Focused Living Series.* Church Resource Ministries, 1996. I was aided in my approach to determining my personal mission statement by this material which has guided my thoughts in this section.

Chapter 9

1. Wolgemuth, Robert. *The Most Important Place on Earth.* Thomas Nelson, 2004. Page 93,95.

Chapter 11

1. Giglio, Louie. *The Comeback.* W Publishing Group, 2015. Page 160.

2. Chambers, Oswald. "Power For Living" in SP Publications. Volume 55, Sept.-Nov. 1997.

3. Notes on Matthew 17:14-20; Luke 17:6

14 When they came to the crowd, a man approached Jesus and knelt before him. 15 "Lord, have mercy on my son," he said. "He has seizures and is suffering greatly. He often falls into the fire or into the water. 16 I brought him to your disciples, but they could not heal him."

17 "You unbelieving and perverse generation," Jesus replied, "how long shall I stay with you? How long shall I put up with you? Bring the boy here to me." 18 Jesus rebuked the demon, and it came out of the boy, and he was healed at that moment.

19 Then the disciples came to Jesus in private and asked, "Why couldn't we drive it out?"

20 He replied, "Because you have so little faith. Truly I tell you, if you have faith as small as a mustard seed, you can say to this mountain, 'Move from here to there,' and it will move. Nothing will be impossible for you." (Matthew 17:14-20 NIV)

The context of Jesus' statement about having "faith the size as a mustard seed" is the disciples come to Jesus about why they could not cast the demon out of the boy. Jesus teaches that "mustard seed" faith accesses God's power. The promise is that there is no limit to God's power in making "all things possible".

He replied, "If you have faith as small as a mustard seed, you can say to this mulberry tree, 'Be uprooted and planted in the sea,' and it will obey you. (Luke 17:6 NIV)

The mulberry tree's roots were regarded as incredibly strong, making it virtually impossible to uproot. "Mustard seed" faith is rewarded by God, making all things possible.

Chapter 12

1. Lucado, Max. *God's Story Your Story*. Zondervan, 2011. Page 25.